VICTORIOUS CHRISTIAN LIVING

E.C NAKELI, PHD

Victorious Christian Living

E. C. Nakeli, PhD

© 2020 by E.C. Nakeli
Published by Perez Publishing

For your questions and publishing needs, write to:
Perez Publishing
40 S Church st
Westminster, MD 21157
E-mail: *ecnakeli@yahoo.com*
Printed in the United States of America
All rights reserved. No part of this publication may be reproduced, stored in a retrieval systems, or transmitted in any form or by any means — for example,
electronic, photocopy, recording — without the prior written permission of the publisher. The only exception is brief quotations in printed reviews.

To contact the author, write to:
E.C. Nakeli
40 S Church st
Westminster, MD 21157
E-mail: *ecnakeli@yahoo.com*

Victorious Christian Living/E.C. Nakeli
ISBN: 9781945055263
Unless otherwise indicated, Scriptures references are from
THE HOLY BIBLE, NEW INTERNATIONAL VERSION®, NIV®
Copyright © 1973, 1978, 1984, 2011 by Biblica, Inc™
Used by permission. All rights reserved worldwide.

Table of Contents

Acknowledgements viii
Dedication ix
chapter 1 12
Understanding the conflict 12
    The Nature of the conflict 13
God's design 15
Heed the Command 16
Only as He Leads 17
The battle is God's 18
Chapter 2 20
Understanding your enemy: his strengths and weaknesses 20
His nature 20
    Your enemy is powerful: 21
    Your enemy is fierce and cruel: 21
Your enemy is malignant: 22
    Your enemy is deceitful: 22
    Your enemy is restless: 23
    Your enemy is daring: 23
    Your enemy is fallen: 24
    Your enemy is disarmed: 25
Chapter 3 26
Understanding your enemy: his activities 26
    He is an accuser 26
    He sows thistles (weeds, tares) 27
    He steals the word 28
    He perverts scriptures 29
    He opposes the work of God 29
    He keeps people bound 30
Chapter 4 32
Our mandate 32
    The enemy has weapons 33
    His weapons are designed for failure 33
    We have a mandate to judge 34
Chapter 5 39
Our weapons of defence 39
What our weapons are not 40
The potentials of our weapons 40

What our weapons are	4
Our weapons of defence	41
General weapons of defence	42
Personal weapons of defence	44
Chapter 6	4
Our weapons of offence	4
Chapter 7	5
Our composure	5
Know the setbacks	6
Another setback	6
Chapter 8	6
Set up for victory	6
Being careful	6
Power in purity	6
Satan knows there is power in purity	70
Keep in phase with the Spirit	7
Be on the offensive	7
How to appropriate the victory	7
chapter 9	7
Your counter strategy	7
Some facts about self-control	7
it is for all believers:	79
it is indispensable for leadership:	80
lack of self-control makes you vulnerable:	80
it prepares you for action:	81
How to acquire self-control	81
Chapter10	8
How to resist the devil	8
Why you should stand firm	90
How to stand firm	9
Chapter 11	9
Slaying the monster	9
(dealing with the greatest limitation)	9
Its manifestations (what sin is)	9
Sin	95
Transgression	97
Trespass	99
Iniquity	99
Chapter 12	101

The destructive power of sin 101
What sin does to a man! 101
A case study 113
    The seal 116
    The cord 117
Chapter 13 119
How to deal with sin 119
Sin must be confessed specifically 120
    How is confession done? 122
Sin must be amended for 125
Chapter 14 127
Knowing who and what you are 127
He will uphold you 130
Chapter 15 138
Wielding your weapons 138

Acknowledgements

I wrote this book back in 2006 and want to thank the youths and entire congregation of Christian Missionary Fellowship International, Kumba Cameroon. During these thirteen years since the book was written, I have been part of two other vibrant congregations, Christian Missionary Fellowship International, Westminster, Maryland, and Christ Gospel City in Karlsruhe, Germany. I want to say thank you to the pastors and members of these congregations. I also want to thank the members, friends, and partners of Gospel Light International Ministries and SEKEL Institutes.

Dedication

I dedicate this book to my children ; my sons Maaseiah Pele and Seraiah Mashal, and my daughter Loria Pristine. May the Lord train your hands for battle. May you learn the secrets of victorious Christian living and become warriors for the Kingdom.

x

chapter 1

Understanding the conflict

T he Christian life is one of continuous conflict for the one who must live up to the standards of God as prescribed in the Book. The Christian faces daily the pressures of sin, the world and the devil himself, which seek to lure away his soul from a true and total allegiance to the King of the universe. No matter the intensity of conflict, the Christian life can be one of continuous victory and triumph over the forces of evil, for the one who seeks to understand the nature of the conflict, understand the enemy, and apply the principles of victory as described in the Bible.

In this study, we are going to do just that; getting to understand the nature of the conflict, the real enemy and seeing how we can apply God's revealed principles or strategy which the believer must use for victory.

The Nature of the conflict

To understand the nature of the conflict we can only turn to God's Handbook for living. As we study it, in my opinion, the following points emerge with respect to the nature of the conflict we are in.

1). **The conflict is universal:**

The universality of the conflict means that there is no exemption as to who is involved. As long as you are human, irrespective of your race, culture, geographical location, vocation or social status you remain a part of the conflict.

"The great dragon was hurled down--that ancient serpent called the devil, or Satan, who leads the whole world astray. He was hurled to the earth, and his angels with him" (Revelations 12:9).

Do you see the qualification given to satan here? One who leads the whole world astray, irrespective of the above-mentioned differences that seem to divide the human race.

The whole world is in a state of war; cognizant or ignorant of the fact. We only do ourselves good when we come to grips with the truth about it and act accordingly. Though the conflict is universal and there are no exemptions, satan has a primary target- the believers. The Bible says, **"Then the dragon was enraged at the woman and went off to make war against the rest of her offspring--those who obey God's commandments and hold to the testimony of Jesus" (Revelations 12:17).**

The devil is still making war against the elect of God all over the world. Knowing this will give you courage to hold on and keep up the fight, **"because you know that your brothers all over the world are undergoing the same kind of sufferings" (1Peter 5:9).**

2). **The conflict is continuous:**
Usually conflicts last for a period of time depending on the scale. However, to the Christian, his entire life is in a "state of war". The battle you are engaged in is a battle of a lifetime, as long as God lends you breath.

The Bible says, **"your enemy the devil prowls around like a roaring lion looking for someone to devour" (1 Peter 5:8).** "Prowls around" is in the present continuous, that is, he is prowling around and will keep prowling around. From ancient times he has been "roaming through the earth and going to and fro in it" (Job1:7). About the Lord Jesus it is written, "when the devil had finished tempting him he left him until an opportue time"(Luke 4:13). Each victory prepares you for the next battle in the conflict.

3). **The conflict is first of all spiritual:**
There are surely physical evidences and manifestations which show that the believer is in conflict with the forces of evil. But, in spite of these physical manifestations, it is necessary to understand that the conflict is first of all spiritual. Knowing this defines your approach to the conflict. The Bible says, **"For our struggle is not against flesh and blood, but against the rulers, against the authorities, against the powers of this dark world and against the spiritual forces of evil in the heavenly realms" (Ephesians 6:12).**

The conflict you are in is not against flesh and blood-human beings-but against spirit beings which may use human agents, in an organized system to propagate evil. That's why we are told, "the weapons we fight with are not the weapons of the world" (2Corinthians 10:4a). Knowing that the conflict is first of all spiritual, we can look at the cause rather than the effect, we can chase the substance rather than the shadow and in doing so, victory can be guaranteed in every battle.

God's design

God has designed that the Christian learns to do battle in this life. It is His commitment to train us to do battle. The Bible teaches us that our God is a "man of war". Like every good father, He wants to teach us to be like Him. It is for this reason He decided to leave us for a while in this enemy territory after we pledged allegiance to His service and to be His representatives and carriers of His banner of victory. He knows that nothing awaits us in this hostile enemy zone where darkness reigns but an endless string of continuous assault from the enemy and his allies who consider those who have pledged allegiance to heaven's King as traitors.

Our heavenly Father, in order to reveal His power and glory to the enemies of our souls, has decided in His sovereignty that He will display this only through us, thus letting the devil and his cohorts to understand that "the earth is[still] the Lord's and everything in it, the world and all who live in it" (Psalm 24:1, emphasis added).

Moses told the Israelites, "when you go to war against your enemies…" (Deuteronomy 20:1). He repeated these same words in this final discourse of his with the children of Israel whom he led out of Egypt and through the wilderness; "when you go to war against your enemies..."(Deuteronomy 21:10). Therefore, warfare is considered to be an integral part of the life of the believer. Moses did not say" if you go to war" but "when you go to war".

The normal Christian life is one of war and when this war is absent from the life of the believer, it can be sure that compromise exists somewhere between that one and the forces of evil. If spiritual warfare is lacking in a life then vitality is also lacking. The degree of victorious warfare determines one's degree of spiritual riches and vitality. Nothing in the Christian life will come on a silver platter. God has designed for you to war for everything you must possess.

The believer must advance into his or her allotted territory else that which is rightly his will remain under enemy occupation. Satan will not give up on anything unless he is forced to. He will not allow you enter the fullness of your inheritance until you have engaged him in battle and dislodged him from every territory of yours he is illegally occupying.

Heed the Command
"The LORD our God said to us at Horeb, "You have stayed long enough at this mountain. [7] Break camp and advance into the hill country of the Amorites; go to all the neighboring peoples in the Arabah, in the mountains, in the western foothills, in the Negev and along the coast, to the land of the Canaanites and to Lebanon, as far as the great river, the Euphrates. [8] See, I have given you this land. Go in and take possession of the land that the LORD swore he would give to your fathers--to Abraham, Isaac and Jacob--and to their descendants after them"(Deuteronomy 1:6-8).

You must advance to possess your possession. God wants you to take possession of all that He has allotted to you. He wants you to possess the plain – those things which appear easy and ordinary. He wants you to possess the mountains – those things which appear difficult and extraordinary. He wants you to possess the dry lands – those things which appear at first sight to offer little or nothing. He wants you to possess the coast – those things which appear to offer much. Nothing must be left for the enemy.

You must go in for all that is yours. This will require active warfare in identifying the strongholds of the enemy in your life and pulling them down, thereby dislodging the enemy. I want you to understand that the land of abundance is also the land of battle. If you must enter the abundant life you must engage every enemy of yours in battle, on your way to the land. Having entered you must keep out the enemy through active warfare in order to enjoy your abundant inheritance.

Only as He Leads

God has also designed that this battle must be fought only as he leads and directs. We must be constantly at His command if we must fight wisely. In the second chapter of the book of Deuteronomy you will find that there are things the Lord will ask you to engage in battle now, others He will ask you to engage in battle later, and others He will ask you to leave alone. You may never understand the reasons why He does it, but you can be sure that the One leading you is leading you to victory.

Another aspect of His design in this battle is that we fight with weapons which are heaven's make. Weapons specially designed with the power, potentials, and precision of heaven. He has not called us to use self-made weapons but those with divine power.

To show the importance God attaches to our practice of warfare, turn with me to the Book:

"These are the nations the LORD left to test all those Israelites who had not experienced any of the wars in Canaan ² (he did this only to teach warfare to the descendants of the Israelites who had not had previous battle experience): ³ the five rulers of the Philistines, all the Canaanites, the Sidonians, and the Hivites living in the Lebanon mountains from Mount Baal Hermon to Lebo Hamath. ⁴ They were left to test the Israelites to see whether they would obey the LORD's commands, which he had given their forefathers through Moses." (Judges 3:1-4)

So God's design for us is that
1. We learn how to do warfare.
2. We prove our allegiance to the Homeland and to our King and Commander-in-chief Christ Jesus through warfare

The battle is God's
Though we have been called into this life of conflict, one thing we must know is that the battle is not ours. We have just been called into it so that as partakers in such a great warfare we are bound to share in the booty, whether we remain with the supply line or we are at the front line leading the pursuit of the enemy. Knowledge that the battle is the Lord's will lead us to understand that the victory is ours. You should have in mind that God will never ask you to go into battle if He will not lead the way. God will not ask you to possess that which He has not given you. God's call into battle comes with a total commitment on His part to make the

impossible possible. It comes with a total commitment on His part to engage and weaken the enemy for you to conquer. This is why He told the Israelites time and again: "the Lord will fight for you; you need only be still" (Exodus 14:14). "Do not be afraid of them; the Lord your God himself will fight for you" (Deuteronomy 3:22). "For the Lord your God is the one who goes with you to fight for you against your enemies to give you victory" (Deuteronomy 20:4)

Chapter 2

Understanding your enemy: his strengths and weaknesses

No one ever goes into a war expecting to win without first understanding the nature of the conflict and the enemy; his nature, strategies and activities. We just talked in the previous chapter about the nature of the conflict. In this section we shall talk about the nature of the enemy.

His nature

The Bible does not leave us in the dark as far as the nature of your enemy is concerned. The very first thing I want to draw your attention to is the fact that the enemy who is fighting against you once was an arch angel of God. He once had access to the immediate presence of God. He existed long before you were born, but is however a creature of God's like you are.

The enemy you are dealing with is not omnipotent, he is not omniscient, he is not omnipresent neither is he self-existent. Like every other created thing he has his being in Christ alone in whom **"all things have their being."** Nevertheless, that does not make him an ant. You must understand his "potentials" to cause harm. The greatest deception in any and every conflict is to underestimate the capabilities of your enemy, and we do not want to get into that trap. Knowing the Following will help you:

Your enemy is powerful:
"For our struggle is not against flesh and blood, but against the rulers, against the authorities, against the powers of this dark world and against the spiritual forces of evil in the heavenly realms" (Ephesians 6:12)

This verse gives you a picture into the nature of the enemy. It presents to us an organized system of evil. Words like "powers' and "forces" give you a picture that you are not in for a joke. I want you to understand that your enemy is powerful; with us humans no one can match his strength.

Your enemy is fierce and cruel:
"For Jesus had commanded the evil spirit to come out of the man. Many times it had seized him, and though he was chained hand and foot and kept under guard, he had broken his chains and had been driven by the demon into solitary places"(Luke 8:29).
"A spirit seizes him and he suddenly screams; it throws him into convulsions so that he foams at the mouth. It scarcely ever leaves him and is destroying him" (Luke 9:39).

Satan and his hosts are no friends to the human race. They will use every opportunity to manifest their fierceness and cruelty to any degree. You are dealing with an enemy whose ultimate intention is to hurt. The Bible says he **"comes only to steal, to kill, and to destroy" (John 10:10)**

Your enemy is malignant:
"when suddenly a mighty wind swept in from the desert and struck the four corners of the house. It collapsed on them and they are dead, and I am the only one who has escaped to tell you" (Job 1:9)!

"Skin for skin!" Satan replied. "A man will give all he has for his own life" (Job 2:4).

You have an enemy who does everything to turn your Father against you. These statements of satan's were not to appreciate God or Job, but were malevolent in intent. His only disposition is to inflict injury and loss.

Your enemy is deceitful:
Put on the whole armour of God, that ye may be able to stand against the wiles of the devil" (Ephesians 6:11, KJV).

"And no wonder, for Satan himself masquerades as an angel of light" (2Corinthians 11:14).

You have a cunning, crafty, deceptive and beguiling enemy. The Bible talks about his wiles. His principal method of operating is through deception; cleverly invented schemes employed to lure away your precious soul. He wouldn't mind to disguise as an angel of light. He wouldn't mind to make seemingly good offers. Remember he used this subtlety against Eve.

"Now the serpent was more crafty than any of the wild animals the LORD God had made. He said to the woman, "Did God really say, `You must not eat from any tree in the garden'?" (Genesis 3:1)
"But I am afraid that just as Eve was deceived by the serpent's cunning, your minds may somehow be led astray from your sincere and pure devotion to Christ" (2Corinthains 11:3).

Satan knows that no one, in his right senses, will ever buy his ideas. Thus, the only way for him to operate and have his way is through craftiness.

Your enemy is restless:
1Peter 5:8 and Job1:7 let us know that satan is restless, always at work. The Lord Jesus Christ, describing him in a parable said, "But while others were sleeping, his enemy came…" (Matthew 13:25)
It tells you your enemy does not sleep, he has no leave. Every other person may rest but not satan the devil. He seeks to invent new ways to accomplish his mission.

Your enemy is daring:
" One day the angels came to present themselves before the LORD, and Satan also came with them" (Job 1:6).

'Then the devil took him to the holy city and had him stand on the highest point of the temple. ⁶ "If you are the Son of God," he said, "throw yourself down"' (Matthew 4:5).

Your enemy is a shamelessly bold creature who even dares to approach the King of the universe to present himself as a son in spite of the fact that he rebelled and refused to repent. Would you for one moment think that he would try, not once nor twice, to deceive the Son of God? There's nothing satan would not attempt in order to get you into his trap. He can be very daring, shamelessly.

Do not overestimate him!

Until now I seem to have presented to you the strengths of your enemy. To better win a war you must seek to understand both the strengths and the weakness of your enemy. As good as it is not to undermine one's enemy, it is better not to magnify him. Understanding his weaknesses gives you directives on where, when and how to strike. Let's look at his weaknesses in the next section.

Your enemy is fallen:
"And there was war in heaven. Michael and his angels fought against the dragon, and the dragon and his angels fought back. 8 But he was not strong enough, and they lost their place in heaven. 9 The great dragon was hurled down--that ancient serpent called the devil, or Satan, who leads the whole world astray. He was hurled to the earth, and his angels with him" (Revelations 12: 7-9).
'He replied, "I saw Satan fall like lightning from heaven"' (Luke 10:18).

Satan's primary target was God, but, because he was no match for the Almighty omnipotent Lord of the hosts of heaven, he was defeated by Archangel Michael and his host of angels. "But he was not strong enough", that is the description of the enemy both then and now. He is not strong enough to battle or stand against the Lord of hosts. I want you to know that he lost his place in heaven; place of authority, prominence or recognition. He is a fallen prince. He was driven "in <u>disgrace</u> from the mount of God" and "expelled from among the fiery stones"(see Ezekiel 28:16, emphasis added) by the Father because of his sin. The only reason he has any mandate on earth is because man gives him a date. If man would refuse to have a date with satan, then the devil will cease to have any operational mandate on planet earth. The same way he was hurled down from heaven to earth is the same way he will be hurled down from earth to the lake of fire.

Your enemy is disarmed:
"And having disarmed the powers and authorities, he made a public spectacle of them, triumphing over them by the cross" (Colossians 2:15).

Satan was disarmed on the cross by the Prince of Peace. He has nothing to harm the saint with but what is foolishly given him by the saint. Just as satan has no authority but what is given him by man, he has no weapon but what man gives him. That is why he seeks the allegiance of man in order to fully operate. He is like a soldier carrying a rifle without cartridges. He may present himself as fully armed, but the truth of the matter is, he isn't armed at all. He can only use what you surrender to him without which he remains powerless. Your enemy may put up a front, but knowledge of the fact that he has been disarmed keeps you from panic.

Chapter 3

Understanding your enemy: his activities

He is an accuser

The Bible refers to him as the accuser of the saints.

"For the accuser of our brothers, who accuses them before our God day and night, has been hurled down" (Revelations 12:10b).

Satan looks for every opportunity to accuse the believer before his heavenly Father. He will stop at nothing to make his case genuine. The Bible says he does so "day and night", referring to the continuous nature of his accusations. We find a good illustration of this in the book of Job and more vividly in the book of Zechariah:

"Then he showed me Joshua the high priest standing before the angel of the LORD, and Satan standing at his right side to accuse him" (Zechariah 3:1).

Why was satan standing there to accuse him? Because he was wearing filthy clothes! Filthy clothes stand for our misdeeds and acts of

unrighteousness; they represent our sins and failures. If there is anything satan would take advantage of, it is when a believer lives carelessly.
Do you remember what the Lord of glory said while on earth? **"I will not speak with you much longer, for the prince of this world is coming. He has no hold on me…" (John 14:30).**

Satan will always come to us, but even if he comes as often as he wants, let him find nothing in us with which to accuse us before the Judge of the universe. Let it be said of you and I that **"True instruction was in his mouth and nothing false was found on his lips. He walked with me in peace and uprightness, and turned many from sin" (Malachi 2:6).**

He sows thistles (weeds, tares)
"But while everyone was sleeping, his enemy came and sowed weeds among the wheat, and went away" (Matthew 13:25).

Weeds, thorns and thistles in scripture represent that which is undesired of God. Anything that is counterfeit and tends to prevent the authentic from thriving is represented by any of the above.
Sin, strife, confusion, quarrelling, hatred, slander, etc are all tares in God's field. These are the handiwork of satan.

However, just like any farmer, satan will not sow his seeds where he knows they cannot grow. We become guilty when our lives become fertile grounds for satan to cultivate his weeds, tares, thorns and thistles. The Bible says that **"Land that drinks in the rain often falling on it and that produces a crop useful to those for whom it is farmed receives the blessing of God. [8] But land that produces thorns and thistles is worthless and is in danger of being cursed. In the end it will be burned" (Hebrews 6:7-8).**

Permit me ask you a question to which you should answer honestly: is your life a fertile ground for satan to cultivate his ills amongst the people of God? Are you a breeding ground for strife, gossip, quarrelling etc.? Have you sold yourself to the devil to be his workshop?

He steals the word
"When anyone hears the message about the kingdom and does not understand it, the evil one comes and snatches away what was sown in his heart. This is the seed sown along the path" (Matthew 13:19). "Those along the path are the ones who hear, and then the devil comes and takes away the word from their hearts, so that they may not believe and be saved" (Luke 8:12).

The path stands for or represents the unprotected heart; the heart that allows just anything to have access into it. You know, just anything can walk on a path; from animals to birds, both clean and unclean. Thus, the path represents the unguarded, unselective heart. Again, the soil on any path is harder than that of the surrounding ground. This also implies the path represents the hardened heart where nothing can penetrate or be hidden in.

It is time to examine your heart to know of what kind it is! Satan has access only to the unguarded and hardened heart. You know he only steals from the heart which does not understand the word that is preached. Understanding is what hides the word in the heart of a man, but when the heart is hardened nothing can be hidden in it.

The Bible says, **"above all else, guard your heart…."** (Proverbs 4:23). Not to heed to this instruction is to give satan free access to steal that which is sown in the heart.

He perverts scriptures

The devil, if he cannot steal the word from the heart, tries to give it a misinterpretation to suit his schemes.

"Then the devil took him to the holy city and had him stand on the highest point of the temple. ⁶ "If you are the Son of God," he said, "throw yourself down. For it is written: " `He will command his angels concerning you, and they will lift you up in their hands, so that you will not strike your foot against a stone" (Matthew 4:5-6).

Think of all the sects which have originated because of misinterpretation and perversion of scriptures. This is nothing other than the handiwork of satan. If he cannot keep you from believing, he will get you to believe his lies which are often based on his perversion of scripture.

He opposes the work of God

"The god of this age has blinded the minds of unbelievers, so that they cannot see the light of the gospel of the glory of Christ, who is the image of God" (2 Corinthians 4:4).

"For we wanted to come to you--certainly I, Paul, did, again and again--but Satan stopped us" (1 Thessalonians 2:18).

From the time the devil was driven out of heaven in total disgrace, he decided that he was going to work against God's plans and purposes for the universe. His first attempt was at Eden when he succeeded to get man to rebel against God. Today he is actively at work trying to prevent the Gospel from spreading to the different parts of the planet. He blinds the mind of people so they wouldn't see the light of the Gospel of Jesus and be saved. He also steals away the word sown in the hearts of men. The devil also stops servants of God, when he can, from carrying this Gospel to new grounds.

He keeps people bound
"Then should not this woman, a daughter of Abraham, whom Satan has kept bound for eighteen long years, be set free on the Sabbath day from what bound her?" (Luke 13:16)

Countless numbers of people have spent a greater part of their lives in satan's prison of torments. Still many are held captive in the kingdom of darkness. In one aspect of their lives or the other they find themselves bound by disease, curses, addictions, poverty, failure, disobedience etc. The devil is a cruel taskmaster who delights in tormenting those who refuse to serve him wholeheartedly. Do you see the number of people bound to one form of addiction or the other? That is the work of satan. Have you seen anyone bound by disease and ill-health? That is the work of satan. Have you seen anyone bound to sensual pleasure? That is the work of satan. Have you seen anyone bound to rebellion? That is the work of satan.

Having exposed the enemy and his activities, the next thing is to see how we can employ our God-given strategies and resources to "obtain" and maintain victory over him. However, to effectively employ these resources you must understand your authority over him. The King of Glory said, **"I have given you authority to trample on snakes and scorpions and to overcome all the power of the enemy; nothing will harm you" (Luke 10:19).**

Remember I said before that satan could only have authority to work on earth because man gave him that authority. Today, his only mandate is because man gives him a date. For the believer, the Lord Jesus has given us the authority He has over both the heavens and the earth. Remember He said, **"All authority in heaven and on earth has been given to me" (Matthew 28:18).**

It is the same authority He gave to us to trample on satan and his works. Ha gave us authority to overcome all the power of the enemy- his power to take away lives, his power to inflict diseases, his power to sow confusion and cause strife, his power to hinder the gospel-yes all his powers. That's the authority you and I have as long as we refuse to have anything to do with him and his works and schemes and ideas. By this we maintain our authority over him.

Chapter 4

Our mandate

"'No weapon forged against you will prevail, and you will refute every tongue that accuses you. This is the heritage of the servants of the LORD, and this is their vindication from me," declares the LORD' (Isaiah 54:17).

"May the praise of God be in their mouths and a double-edged sword in their hands, to inflict vengeance on the nations and punishment on the peoples, to bind their kings with fetters, their nobles with shackles of iron, to carry out the sentence written against them. This is the glory of all his saints" (Psalm 149:5-9).

We said that God has designed for us to fight and possess all what He has ordained for us from before the foundations of the world. We said He has also designed that He must lead every step of the battle. He has equally designed the weapons we must use in this battle. Everything in this battle originates from Him, is carried out in Him and ends in Him. Now, I want you to understand our mandate as sons of God and co-heirs with Christ as far as this conflict is concerned. From our verse above in Isaiah we can immediately bring out the following:

The enemy has weapons
"no weapon forged against you…"

The devil does not use his weapons randomly; they are specially forged (designed, empowered and directed against) different individuals in different circumstances as the need may be. The weapons he used against you yesterday are not the same weapons he will use against you today. He seeks to upgrade and adapt those weapons through information given him by monitoring spirits, cameras and spiritual spy satellites he has placed to monitor you. He even has human agents who may appear as close friends who feed him with information concerning you.

His weapons are designed for failure
"No weapon forged against you shall prevail"

The outcome of everything that happens here on planet earth and the whole wide universe is determined not by the devil but by God. God has the final word on all that happens in this universe. What He permits takes place and what he does not permit can never take place. He has determined that no matter how sophisticated the enemy may design his weapons, none of them will accomplish their intended purpose. They may be designed, they may be launched against us, they may reach us, but one thing is sure; that their purpose for which they were designed and launched will never be accomplished. It is as if this were an eternal curse the Lord has placed on all the weapons of the enemy. The ill-intentions of his weapons will be transformed by the Almighty Sovereign Lord into His good purpose.

We have a mandate to judge
"…and you will refute every tongue that accuses you"

God has given us the mandate to refute or to judge and condemn every tongue that raises accusations against us before the throne room of God's justice. We have the mandate to counter petition satan. We have the mandate to judge and condemn all incantations, mutterings, enchantments, curses and all what the enemy and his human agents may throw at us. From our passage in Psalms we can bring out the following:

1. **God has given us an honour**

"Let the saints rejoice in this honour"

The honour is that He has chosen the same ones whom the devil deceived and enslaved to be the very ones, weak as we are in ourselves, through whom He will accomplish His eternal plan and purposes. He has given us the honour to exercise His authority and His power over principalities, powers, and hosts of wickedness. It is an honour for mortal man to be engaged in supernatural conflict and still emerge victorious. This is the design of our Father, God Almighty.

2. We have the mandate to inflict vengeance

"...to inflict vengeance on the nations"

The nations here refer to the enemies of God's people which are satan together with his spirit and human agents. We have the mandate to execute heaven's vengeance on all those attacking the work and the people of God. That is why the Lord Jesus Christ said **"I have given you authority to trample on snakes and scorpions and to overcome all the power of the enemy; nothing will harm you" (Luke 10:19).**

When you come in contact with a snake or a scorpion, the first reaction is to slay it. We are called to trample all the works and power of the enemy. We execute vengeance by blocking, frustrating, and bringing to naught all his schemes, devices and plans. We execute vengeance by pulling down his strongholds and fortresses. We execute vengeance by limiting and restricting his area of operation. We execute vengeance by forcing him to flee.

3. We have the mandate to punish

"...and punishment on the peoples"

One way to punish somebody, I mean the most effective way, is to destroy the fruits of that person's labour ensuring that, that one never reaps the benefits of his labour. It is to allow the person work with nothing to show for all his work. If we are to execute judgement on satan and his cohorts, then we must judge and destroy all that he plants.

We execute judgement by forcing him to let go his captives, yes by bringing deliverance to those he has chained and enslaved. It is by forcing him to pack out of places he is claiming illegal ownership. We execute judgement on him by placing and enforcing heaven's restraining orders on his activities. **"And we will be ready to punish every act of disobedience…" (2Corinthians10:6).**

Let us execute judgement on his works by breaking curses, healing the sick, delivering the oppressed and ensuring that nothing of his prospers in and around us.

4. <u>We have the mandate to bind</u>

"To bind their kings with fetters, their nobles with shackles of iron"

When you bind someone, you restrict that one's activities, movements and other possibilities of exercising his free will. We have been given the mandate to restrict the activities of the rulers of darkness by binding them. We need not be able to see them with our physical eyes and bind them with our physical hands. As kings, that which we declare with our lips is put into effect, as we declare it by faith in the name of Jesus Christ.

As we declare it God's holy angels execute the orders. Until they are bound, they remain loose and free to move about and operate. There are moments when I have commanded demons to be bound hand, neck, and foot together putting them in the most painful condition especially when they have proven stubborn. God has given us the mandate to bind, let us put it to use and frustrate the activities of satan and his cohorts in our individual lives, our environment, and our churches.

5. We have the mandate to implement heaven's decision

"To carry out the sentence written against them"

We, the children of God, are the sheriff-bailiffs of our Father's Kingdom which governs the whole universe. We are charged with the responsibility to implement what heaven's court has written against the criminals of the universe- satan and his demons. I read a book in which an occult grand master arrested by Jesus and now serving Him said that they were made to believe that us believers are the most wanted psychic criminals who must be arrested and destroyed.

The devil is indeed a liar! The Lord Jesus Christ calls him the thief who comes only to steal, to kill, and to destroy. Heaven's judgement is that satan is a thief (John 10:10), a murderer (John 8:44), a liar (John 8:44), an usurper (Isaiah 14:13-14) and a deceiver (Revelation 13:14). Let us execute the sentences written against him as a thief:

"A thief must certainly make restitution, but if he has nothing, he must be sold to pay for his theft" (Exodus 22:3b).

"Men do not despise a thief if he steals to satisfy his hunger when he is starving. Yet if he is caught, he must pay sevenfold, though it costs him all the wealth of his house" (Proverbs 6:30-31).

We must command him to obey heaven's court order and restore whatever he has stolen, whether from you or your relative or your brethren. Identify specific things and compel him in the name of Jesus to restore them sevenfold. Identify things in your environment which he has stolen and command him to restore them sevenfold. That is heaven's decision and he has no option but to obey.

You can also execute other sentences like **"The wicked shall be turned into hell, and all the nations that forget God » (Psalm 9:17, KJV) and "For if God did not spare angels when they sinned, but sent them to hell, putting them into gloomy dungeons to be held for judgment" (2Peter 2:4).** Remind them of where they belong and where they are supposed to be. They have no claim on earth for it was initially given to man to inhabit and fill and not for demons to infiltrate and occupy. Fallen angels are supposed to be bound in gloomy dungeons in hell. Their invasion of earth and the havoc they are causing in the lives of people are illegal. Remind them of the final judgement which awaits them:

"And the devil, who deceived them, was thrown into the lake of burning sulfur, where the beast and the false prophet had been thrown. They will be tormented day and night for ever and ever" (Revelation 20:10).

"Then death and Hades were thrown into the lake of fire. The lake of fire is the second death" (Revelation 20:14).

Chapter 5

Our weapons of defence

"The weapons we fight with are not the weapons of the world. On the contrary, they have divine power to demolish strongholds" (2Corinthians 10:4).

"The weapons we fight with…"

This clearly shows that there are weapons we are to use in this conflict. This is not just a conflict of attitudes or words, but that which involves real weapons. I want you to take note that the weapons are in the plural, meaning there are many weapons both in type and numbers. In fighting we need both weapons of defence and weapons of offence. We said earlier that God has designed weapons for us to use in this battle as He leads us.

What our weapons are not
"The weapons we fight with are not the weapons of the world"

"The weapons of our warfare are not carnal" (KJV)

Think of all the weapons of war you can imagine, from the most rudimentary to the most sophisticated. In this warfare we are engaged in, none of those weapons will work. That is why we do not take up arms in order for us to propagate the gospel of Jesus. Physical guns will do satan and his demons no harm. The weapons we use cannot be seen with the natural eye nor touched with the physical hands. You can't get into an arms store to purchase any. You cannot order them from Russia, France, Britain, or Iran. They are not the weapons of the flesh; slander, quarrels, cheating, brutality etc.; all such things will instead hinder one's effectiveness in this battle.

The potentials of our weapons
"They have divine power to demolish strongholds"

The weapons we use are invisible weapons with the power of God in them. They are packed loaded with power and capability to demolish every satanic stronghold wherever it may be. Whether in the air, on land, in the sea, beneath the earth, beneath the sea or in outer space.

These weapons have a special penetrating power to burst through any defence system the enemy might erect undetected and unhindered. If nothing can stop the Lord, then nothing can stop this God-manufactured, divinely empowered weapons put at our disposal. However, we must be properly trained to be able to put these weapons to efficient and effective use. No matter the potentials of a weapon, if the one using it has no mastery of its use, it will accomplish nothing or may even backfire on him.

The psalmist said, **"He trains my hands for battle; my arms can bend a bow of bronze" (Psalm 18:34).**

"Praise be to the LORD my Rock, who trains my hands for war, my fingers for battle" (Psalm 144:1).

Each one of us must enrol in God's school of spiritual warfare and go through the training given to us by the Holy Spirit. It is however a school from which nobody graduates in this life. You can only make progress. With each passing day the Holy Spirit will reveal to you new strategies of war and lay at your disposal every new weapon you need for every stage of the conflict. The one who must learn the lessons is the one who is ready to obey every instruction from the Commander- in -chief. You must make yourself totally available to God in this battle.

What our weapons are

We said earlier that we have both weapons of defence and weapons of offence. A victorious army is strong both in the defensive and in the offensive. Any defect in one of the above areas will mean susceptibility to defeat.

Our weapons of defence

The Lord has put at our disposal several weapons of defence which we can separate into general weapons of defence and personal weapons of defence.

By general weapons, I mean those things which the Lord, in His sovereignty, makes available through a simple act of faith to all those who are His; anyone who names the name of the Lord. Daily you can get up and simply claim them through faith.

By personal weapons of defence, I mean those things which the Lord has put at the disposal of the believer through acts of obedience. The believer has the responsibility to put them on. The general can be considered to work even for a group but the personal is for individuals. Several people can be engaged in a battle, some sustain injuries while others do not, depending not only on their fighting skills, but on their weapons of defence.

General weapons of defence
1. The blood of the Lamb

The blood of the Lamb can be used as a covering by the believer. You have to pray and ask the Lord to cover you with the blood of Jesus. Often as I go to bed or get into the day I ask the Lord to cover me with a sea of the blood of the Lamb. A parallel to this is seen in the case of the Israelites in the night of their departure from Egypt when the Lord ask them to use the blood so the destroying angel will pass over them. Those who have come out of satanism have often testified of finding believers covered with a sea of blood such that they cannot be reached.

2. Fire

"And I myself will be a wall of fire around it,' declares the LORD, `and I will be its glory within" (Zechariah 2:5).

The Lord has promised to be a wall of fire round about all those who are His. You will have to daily appropriate this means of defence by faith.

Let us turn to another scripture passage from which we shall get other weapons of defence.

"I love you, O LORD, my strength. The LORD is my rock, my fortress and my deliverer; my God is my rock, in whom I take

refuge. He is my shield and the horn" of my salvation, my stronghold" (Psalm 18:1-2).

3. *The Lord your rock*

Daily you will have to claim the Lord as the rock on which you stand as you fight this battle. You can claim Him as the rock on which you lean as you wage the war against enemy forces. Standing on the rock does not only give you a sure footing, but also sets you high above the enemies which surround you.

4. *The Lord your fortress*

A fortress is a mighty, highly fortified safe haven from every from of attack by the enemy. The one who stays in a fortress and launches attacks from there is beyond the reach of the weapons of his opponents. Appropriate the Lord daily as your fortress.

5. *The Lord your shield*

"But you are a shield around me, O LORD; you bestow glory on me and lift up my head" (Psalm 3:3).

Claim the Lord as your shield daily, to the left, to the right, to the front, and to the back, above and below you. Recall that just as the Lord is unchanging so the shield that He is to you does not wear out. All you have to do is the claim the presence of that shield of defence all around you.

6. *The Lord your stronghold*

A stronghold is a fortress on a smaller scale, but offers the same protection in that, like a fortress it is not easily accessible to the enemy.

7. *The feathers of the Lord*

"Surely he will save you from the fowler's snare and from the deadly pestilence. He will cover you with his feathers, and under

his wings you will find refuge; his faithfulness will be your shield and rampart" (Psalm 91:3-4).**

Like a chick finds shelter and protection under the feathers and wings of the mother hen, so you can find shelter under the wings of the Lord. You can ask the Lord to cover you with His wings and shield you from the attacks of the enemy. It is your right as a child of God, but you must appropriate it daily.

8. *The angels of the Lord*

"If you make the Most High your dwelling--even the LORD, who is my refuge-- then no harm will befall you, no disaster will come near your tent. For he will command his angels concerning you to guard you in all your ways" (Psalm 91: 9-11).

As an envoy of the Kingdom to this world you are entitled to body guards from your homeland. They have the responsibility to protect you from all harm. You just have to acknowledge, daily, your need for them and give them the accord to protect you.

Now that we have looked at the general weapons of defence, it is time we turn to the personal weapons of defence.

Personal weapons of defence

1. *The belt of truth*

"Stand firm then, with the belt of truth buckled around your waist" (Ephesians 6:14a).

The believer's commitment to know, speak and walk in the truth is a personal weapon of defence against the deceptions of the devil. Your love for, and your commitment to truth, puts off the enemy's arrows of deceit. Nothing exposes you to the attacks of the evil one like falsehood in all its manifestations. Unless you are committed to truth you will end up in the fangs of the great serpent of deception. The Bible says

> **"The coming of the lawless one will be in accordance with the work of Satan displayed in all kinds of counterfeit miracles, signs and wonders, [10] and in every sort of evil that deceives those who are perishing. They perish because they refused to love the truth and so be saved." (2 Thessalonians 2:9-10)**

2. The breastplate.

The breastplate is a metal plate worn on the chest to protect the thoracic cavity and the organs therein. There are two kinds of breastplate you must put on:

i. the breastplate of righteousness

> **"With the breastplate of righteousness in place" (Ephesians 6:14b)**

A commitment to and practice of righteousness gives you protection to the vital organs of your spiritual life. Just like you have a physical heart and lungs, so you have a spiritual heart and lungs. Your practice of righteousness will ward of all enemy arrows directed to these vital organs that sustain you spiritually.

ii. The breastplate of love

> **"But since we belong to the day, let us be self-controlled, putting on faith and love as a breastplate, and the hope of salvation as a helmet." (1 Thessalonians 5:8)**

Your commitment to the practice of love as described in 1Corinthians 13 will also act as a breastplate to protect your spiritual vital organs. Love is a sure defence against all kinds of enemy arrows. Love is the key to staying spiritually vibrant.

3. *The boots of the gospel.*

   "And with your feet fitted with the readiness that comes from the gospel of peace" (Ephesians 6:15).

You need boots to be able to walk and run in this battle field of ours. Our Lord said we shall trample on snakes and scorpions. To trample on them bare footed is to take unnecessary risk. Our readiness to preach the gospel is the boots we need in order to safely trample on the snakes and scorpions we have been given mandate to trample. Your degree of readiness to preach the gospel determines how solid and fitting your boots are.

4. *The shield of faith.*

   "In addition to all this, take up the shield of faith, with which you can extinguish all the flaming arrows of the evil one" (Ephesians 6:16).

When it comes to faith acting as a shield, no body's faith can work for you in providing you with this weapon. Faith in God, faith in the finished work of the cross, faith in what God says you are, faith in the promises of God and in your victory over satan will act as a mighty shield wielded against the evil arrows sent against you, stopping and extinguishing all the fiery darts of the enemy.

5. *The helmet.*

    i. *The helmet of salvation.*

      "Take up the helmet of salvation..." (Ephesians 6:17a).
      "But since we belong to the day, let us be self-controlled, putting on faith and love as a breastplate, and the hope of salvation as a helmet" (1Thessalonians 5:8).

The purpose of the helmet is to protect our mind from all forms of enemy assault. Hope is this helmet of salvation! Hope that one day your body shall be redeemed, hope to see your Saviour and Lord, hope for your home in heaven. Hope that one day you will be totally free from all the attacks of satan and his hosts; all this will act as a protective covering over your mind from every invading thought from the enemy to discourage you and cause you to be depressed.

ii. **The helmet of the fruit of the Spirit.**

"Gilead is mine, and Manasseh is mine; Ephraim is my helmet, Judah my scepter" (Psalm 60:7).

The Lord said Ephraim is His helmet. Now, Ephraim means to be twice fruitful. For us, we are expected to bear the fruit of the Spirit. As we bear the fruit of the Spirit, it will provide us with a protective covering over our mind. If you take a careful look at the fruit of the Spirit you will notice that the opposite of each is a vice. Vices provide open doors to demonic attacks, because they represent the works of the flesh which are safe havens for the enemy in the mind that harbours them.

Now that we've examined our weapons of defence, let us take a look at or arsenal of offense in the next chapter.

Chapter 6

Our weapons of offence

1) ***The name of the Lord:***

Every weapon you use in this warfare is only effective in the name of the Lord Jesus. However, the name of the Lord is in itself a mighty weapon against the enemy. It incapacitates him and leaves him dumbfounded. The mention of that name in faith causes him (satan) to do what he hates the most, bow down to Jesus. We might not see it but it happens all the same in the spirit realm.

The psalmist made use of this name against his enemies when he said

> **"All the nations surrounded me, but in the name of the LORD I cut them off. They surrounded me on every side, but in the name of the LORD I cut them off. They swarmed around me like bees, but they died out as quickly as burning thorns; in the name of the LORD I cut them off" (Psalm 118:10-13).**

One night as I slept, I dreamt and was attacked by a group of witches (most often what you dream is actually taking place in the spirit realm). I had no weapon to use and all I did was to quote the above verses and all of them fled. Immediately I got up, I tried finding the scripture I had used but couldn't until several weeks later. There is tremendous power released each time that name is mentioned from a heart of faith and under the anointing.

Sometimes the Lord will want us to use other weapons in His name and at other times He'd rather we just mention that name in faith and the desired results will be produced. This is what the Lord told me about His name on the third day of a twenty-one day fast I took:

"If you are not bold and courageous in life you will be forced to flee when there is actually nothing to flee from. If you do not make up your mine to confront and face challenges, many a time you will have to run from an imaginary enemy. Do not measure an enemy and his capabilities from afar. Be bold enough to challenge even at a close range. If you will stand on My name and on nothing else, your enemies will flee. If you will depend on me and trust wholly on My strength, the shadows which come to frighten will disappear. Stand in the power of My name and be bold to address your mountains. My name is the greatest weapon you have because everything bows and submits to My name. Everything means everything without exception. Quietly use my name! Use it with a low voice! Use My name with a shout! It releases all the power you can ever think of! It causes mountains to flee! It causes doors to open! It shall cause darkness to disappear! There is tremendous power in My name, use it!

2) *Praise in the mouth:*

"May the praise of God be in their mouths and a double-edged sword in their hands" (Psalm 149:6).

Praise, thanksgiving and worship are weapons in the hands of the believer. The praise has to be in the mouth and not in the heart. In other words unless you speak out the praise to God, though your heart may be filled with praise it will do no harm to the enemy. There are too many people who desire to praise but do not praise. Until the praise has reached your lips and is going out into the air it does no harm to the enemy, though God will receive even that which leaves your heart directly to the throne.

Praise spoken out sets the Lord and His holy angels into battle against the forces of darkness. Do you remember what Jehoshaphat and the Israelite army did when confronted by a mighty enemy army? They just praised the Lord and that was enough to set the Lord in battle against that vast army which brought about a victory to the army of Judah.

Often, I have employed this weapon during deliverance sessions, especially when the demons have proven stubborn and all else seem not to work. A song of praise to the Lord sends them packing out through whatever door they can find.

3) *The double- edged sword:*

"May the praise of God be in their mouths and a double-edged sword in their hands" (Psalm 149:6).

"Take the helmet of salvation and the sword of the Spirit, which is the word of God" (Ephesians 6:17).

This is another mighty weapon to the pulling down of satanic strongholds deeply entrenched in our minds, lives and environment. The victorious believer is the one who has mastered the use of this weapon against the devil and his activities. If you learn to answer the devil with the word of God spoken with faith, he will be forced to bow down in every circumstance. In my involvement in deliverance I have discovered that when I counter the claims of demons over those they inhabit, with the word of God their stubbornness is broken. They are forced to give up their claims to a position where they want to negotiate. As I persist with scripture they are forced to a position of pleading and finally forced to flee.

Usually, I do not plan what scripture to use in advance, but the Holy Spirit just causes the appropriate scripture stored within me to spring forth as the need may be. Demons are very crafty! They will want to get you into a position of arguing with them. If you give in to this seduction to use human logic and reason to counter their claims, you will be defeated. Remember they are masters at lies telling. The victorious Christian is the one whose heart is loaded with the word of God. Your attitude towards the word will determine how strong or how weak you are!

4) **The horn of salvation:**

"He has raised up a horn of salvation for us in the house of his servant David" (Luke 1:69).

"He is my shield and the horn of my salvation, my stronghold" (Psalm 18:2c).

The strength of a bull or a buffalo (and any other horned animal) is in their horns. If the Lord is the horn of your salvation then He is the strength with which you can gore the enemy and his works. The living Bible translates that portion of the psalm as "He is my shield. He is like the strong horn of a mighty fighting bull »

5) *The east wind:*

I have asked the Lord several times to release His east wind to sweep away the works of the enemy. I ask Him to release His east wind in specific circumstances when I perceive that the most devastating effect will be produced by this wind just like a hurricane will do in the natural. I have often released the east wind of the Lord to pull down satanic spy cameras, satellites, antennas used by satan and his agents to monitor particular situations. These are a few scriptures out of the many which show how the east wind works against the enemy:

> **"By warfare and exile you contend with her--with his fierce blast he drives her out, as on a day the east wind blow." (Isaiah 27:8).**
>
> **"The east wind carries him off, and he is gone; it sweeps him out of his place. It hurls itself against him without mercy as he flees headlong from its power. It claps its hands in derision and hisses him out of his place" (Job 27:21-23).**
>
> **"Your oarsmen take you out to the high seas. But the east wind will break you to pieces in the heart of the sea" (Ezekiel 27:26).**

6) *Thunder*:

Here, in Africa (and other parts of the world, may be), witches attack their enemies using thunder. Satan just tries his best to mimic that which God does. As you read the Bible, you realise that, thnder is one of the weapons the Lord used often against the enemies of Israel to rout, scatter, and send them fleeing. He used it to judged Egypt and her gods.
This same weapon has been made available to you to use in judging the works of satan, his demons, human agents and why not the devil himself? There are moments when I have asked the Lord to release His thunder

against the enemy forces involved in a particular situation. You may not hear the thunder but I know it happens all the same in the spiritual, affecting the particular situation concerned. Some scriptures which show how this works are given below:

> **"Then the LORD said to Moses, "Stretch out your hand toward the sky so that hail will fall all over Egypt--on men and animals and on everything growing in the fields of Egypt." [23] When Moses stretched out his staff toward the sky, the LORD sent thunder and hail, and lightning flashed down to the ground. So the LORD rained hail on the land of Egypt; [24] hail fell and lightning flashed back and forth. It was the worst storm in all the land of Egypt since it had become a nation. [25] Throughout Egypt hail struck everything in the fields--both men and animals; it beat down everything growing in the fields and stripped every tree" (Exodus 9:22-25).**
>
> **"Those who oppose the LORD will be shattered. He will thunder against them from heaven; the LORD will judge the ends of the earth" (1 Samuel 2:10).**
>
> **"But at your rebuke the waters fled, at the sound of your thunder they took to flight" (Psalm 104:7).**
>
> **"At the thunder of your voice, the peoples flee; when you rise up, the nations scatter" (Isaiah 33:3).**

7) *Lightning*:

Just as natural lightning can cause untold real damage, so lightning in the spiritual can cause damage. When you release, or better still, when you ask the Lord to release lightning in the spiritual against the enemy, it routs him and his cohorts in the situation concerned and victory is won. It destroys their weapons and strategy. The Lord often used lightning against His enemies as seen below:

> **"He shot arrows and scattered the enemies, bolts of lightning and routed them" (2Samuel 22:15)**
>
> **"Send forth lightning and scatter the enemies; shoot your arrows and rout them" (Psalm 144:6).**

8) *Fire:*

Another weapon you can effectively use against the enemy and his works is fire. The Bible says our God is a consuming fire. When we release the fire of the Lord, it sets ablaze the targeted enemy or the targeted works of the enemy in both the spiritual and the natural through the effects it accomplishes. It is written that,

> **"Now the people complained about their hardships in the hearing of the LORD, and when he heard them his anger was aroused. Then fire from the LORD burned among them and consumed some of the outskirts of the camp. ² When the people cried out to Moses, he prayed to the LORD and the fire died down. ³ So that place was called Taberah, because fire from the LORD had burned among them" (Numbers 11:1-3).**
>
> **"Fire went out from Heshbon, a blaze from the city of Sihon. It consumed Ar of Moab, the citizens of Arnon's heights" (Numbers 21:28) .**
>
> **"But be assured today that the LORD your God is the one who goes across ahead of you like a devouring fire. He will destroy**

> them; he will subdue them before you. And you will drive them out and annihilate them quickly, as the LORD has promised you" (Deuteronomy 9:3).

> "Elijah answered the captain, "If I am a man of God, may fire come down from heaven and consume you and your fifty men!" Then fire fell from heaven and consumed the captain and his men" (2kings 1:10).

Once, we were carrying out deliverance, I commanded the fire of the Lord upon the demons. One girl started screaming. After the deliverance session she complained that we had burned her with fire. You see, what we command actually takes place in the spiritual though our physical eyes may not perceive it.

There are spiritual structures of war all around us used by the enemy to launch his attacks at us. As we command the fire of the Lord to fall on these structures, they are actually set ablaze and no satanic fire extinguisher or fire fighter can put out the flame ignited under the Holy Spirit's anointing. That is why after praying certain prayers you receive such violent retaliation from the devil. The fire of the Holy Ghost released in the camp of the enemy will cause untold damage.

9) *The arrows of the Lord:*

> "He shot his arrows and scattered the enemies, great bolts of lightning and routed them" (Psalm 18:14).

> "Send forth lightning and scatter the enemies; shoot your arrows and rout them" (Psalm 144:6).

You can also make use of the arrows of the Lord when you have specific enemy targets to aim at. Spiritual arrows are just like physical arrows; there are things in the physical which you cannot use an arrow to attack, so too in the spiritual. Making use of an arrow depends largely on the target. There are birds of prey, and animals too, which the enemy uses in the spiritual to attack what you have planted. Against such you can make use of the arrows of the Lord. You can also use arrows against human agents of the devil troubling your life. There is what we call the arrow of the Lord (see 2kings 13:15-17), when it is released your victory is guaranteed.

10) *The angels of the Lord*:

God, in His goodness has placed at our disposal, and may I humbly say at our command, angels of war of different ranks so we can make use of them in this spiritual warfare. It is our responsibility to engage them against enemy forces. The Bible says, **"The angel of the Lord encamps around those who fear him" (Psalm 34:7).** Why do they encamp? Primarily to protect and secondarily to receive instructions from us.

I have often asked for commandos from heaven to intervene in particular situations where human intervention is impossible, to get into enemy prisons and set free those held in satanic bondage and dungeons.

David made use of angels when he prayed that, **"May they be like chaff before the wind, with the angel of the LORD driving them away; may their path be dark and slippery, with the angel of the LORD pursuing them" (Psalm 35:5-6).** They can accomplish in the split of a second what you may not accomplish should you be given the whole of eternity. Do you remember what a single angel did to the Syrian army in just one night? **"Then the angel of the LORD went out and put to death a hundred and eighty-five thousand men in the Assyrian camp. When the people got up the next morning--there were all the dead bodies!"**

(Isaiah 37:36). You can ask the Lord to release a band of destroying angels against the enemy forces surrounding you. Learn to make use of this mighty weapon at your disposal, and victory is surely yours.

11) Hailstones

"The LORD threw them into confusion before Israel, who defeated them in a great victory at Gibeon. Israel pursued them along the road going up to Beth Horon and cut them down all the way to Azekah and Makkedah. ¹¹ As they fled before Israel on the road down from Beth Horon to Azekah, the LORD hurled large hailstones down on them from the sky, and more of them died from the hailstones than were killed by the swords of the Israelites" (Joshua 10:10-11).

You can ask the Lord to release hail stones against stubborn enemy forces. Once you ask believe that it is done and visualize the hailstones landing on the heads of your enemies.

12) Drought

This one should be used mostly against water spirits. They cannot withstand drought of any form. If you sense that the situation you are facing involves water spirits, then ask the Lord to release drought upon their environment.

"A drought on her waters! They will dry up. For it is a land of idols, idols that will go mad with terror" (Jeremiah 50:38).

Hezekiah applied this principle when he was under siege by the Assyrians; he diverted the water course so the Assyrians will not find water. There was no way the enemy forces could lay a prolonged siege without water being available to the soldiers.

Do you remember the case of three kings mentioned in 2 Kings 3, how they could not find water after a seven-day march and then concluded that unless the Lord performed a miracle for them, they were in for defeat? Drought is a powerful weapon against the enemy forces especially when it comes to battling against marine spirits.

13). *The blood of the Lamb*

"And they overcame him by the blood of the Lamb, and by the word of their testimony" (Revelations 12:11).

The blood of the Lamb is not only a weapon of defence, but also a very strong weapon of offence. Use the blood of the Lamb against the formation of the forces of evil arrayed against you. Sometimes all you need to say is "the blood of Jesus against you".

14). *The Word of your testimony*

The word of your testimony is another powerful weapon against enemies like doubt, depression, disappointment, fear etc. As you recount the good ness of the Lord towards you, what He has done for you in the past, and what you believe He will do for you, your enemies are weakened and defeated.

Chapter 7

Our composure

The victorious soldier is one who gets into battle cognizant of both his strengths and weaknesses, that is, both his weak points and his strong points. Both must be known and well-guarded in order to be better placed to fight. Also, your approach to the battle will determine whether you win or lose no matter how sophisticated your weapons may be.

The first thing you must understand in this battle is that you are fighting from a position of victory. The Bible says,

"…which he exerted in Christ when he raised him from the dead and seated him at his right hand in the heavenly realms, [21] far above all rule and authority, power and dominion, and every title that can be given, not only in the present age but also in the one to come. [22] And God placed all things under his feet and appointed him to be head over everything for the church, [23] which is his

body, the fullness of him who fills everything in every way…And God raised us up with Christ and seated us with him in the heavenly realms in Christ Jesus" (Ephesians 1:20-23, 2:6).

If you are seated with Christ in heavenly places, and Christ is far above principalities and powers, then you are also above principalities and powers. Your understanding of this truth will determine whether you will be bold and courageous or cower before the enemy.

Know the setbacks
"For God hath not given us the spirit of fear; but of power, and of love, and of a sound mind" (2Timothy 1:7, KJV).

God has given you a spirit of power, love, and a sound mind, and not of fear. The apostle in contrasting the negative quality of fear with three positive qualities is saying that where fear is present the three contrasting qualities will be absent. Nobody who harbours fear can truly demonstrate the Holy Ghost power, neither can he show love nor be in possession of a sound mind.

If you must maintain a victor's disposition there are two things you must deal with at the personal level; fear and discouragement. You will have to do with fear of man. Fear of the future. Fear of failure. Fear of loss. Fear of rejection. Fear of the unknown. Some of the above fears may appear genuine, but they will however prevent you from entering into a victorious life of possessing all that God has in store for you.

Now, I hear someone asking how he or she may deal with her fears. First of all, understand the source of fear; that fear is not of God but of the devil. When you feel fear coming over you, rise and rebuke it in the mighty name of Jesus and claim the boldness that God has offered you by the power of the Holy Ghost. The Bible says, "The righteous are as bold as a lion" (Proverbs 28:1).

Fear is a spirit, as you address it using 2Timothy 1:7 quoted above, personalize it. That is what will give you victory over fear. Also, focus on God and trust His faithfulness. Have in mind that God will never ask you to get into anything if He will not go with you and lead the way. He will not ask you to possess what He has not given you.

God's call into battle comes with a commitment on His part to do the impossible. It comes with a total commitment to engage, weaken and defeat the enemy for you to conquer. Fear in your life will block your view of God's commitment, magnify the difficulties and magnify the potentials of the enemy. It gives you a diminished view, not only of yourself, but also of your God. Fear prevents the release of one's potentials and incapacitates even the most capable.

Second, you must do away with discouragement of any form. The chief forms of discouragement are impatience and the refusal to stretch beyond one's comfort zone. Also, engaging the enemy in your own strength will result in discouragement. In every battle against the enemy there is a part that God plays for victory to be won and only Him can do it. When you try to do that which only God can do, you meet with utmost discouragement.

Throughout Israel's war journey we hear Moses, several times, making statements like "And the Lord will do to them …"

"The Lord will deliver them to you …"

Other sources of fear and discouragement are
- Criticism
- Cynicism

- Lack of faith and trust
- Concentrating on the problem rather than on God.

Anytime you give in to fear you forfeit your victory. When you refuse to believe and trust God, fear takes over your heart. Inner strength and courage are essential to living victoriously. Fear paralyzes, courage catalyzes! At any given time, what God requires of you is a heart that is strong and courageous. Fear and discouragement are outlets to strength, power and soundness of mind. What will maintain your inner strength and courage is knowing that:

(i) God goes ahead of you in every battle
(ii) God will be with you in every battle
(iii) God will never leave nor forsake you.

Another setback

"The officers shall say to the army: "Has anyone built a new house and not dedicated it? Let him go home, or he may die in battle and someone else may dedicate it. 6 Has anyone planted a vineyard and not begun to enjoy it? Let him go home, or he may die in battle and someone else enjoy it. 7 Has anyone become pledged to a woman and not married her? Let him go home, or he may die in battle and someone else marry her." 8 Then the officers shall add, "Is any man afraid or fainthearted? Let him go home so that his brothers will not become disheartened too." 9 When the officers have finished speaking to the army, they shall appoint commanders over it." (Deuteronomy 20:5-9)

Another great possible hindrance to the victories Christian life is distraction. And here above we find several legitimate reasons why a person may go into war distracted. It is better; a million times better, not to wage any war than to engage your enemy with a divided attention. One person with all his focus on a war is far stronger than a hundred people with half a focus on the war.

"Has anyone built a house … has any one planted a vineyard … let him go home"

In these words, we find a great hindrance to spiritual warfare. Many people who may wish they were all-out into spiritual warfare do not do so because of their investments in this life. They are afraid to attack the enemy or else suffer loss. It is good to invest, but if that investment will take the least of your attention, you are made vulnerable to defeat. Things which bring distraction may well be genuine. However, they will limit your capacity to make yourself totally available to your master.

If you search Christian history, you will find that those who have been mightily involved in spiritual warfare and emerge victorious have been those with little or no investments in this life. They often have been people with little or no recognition in society, but before whom all of hell trembles when they get down on their knees.

"Has anyone become pledged to a woman … let him go home …"
Here, we find again another principle to be considered for effectiveness in spiritual warfare. Our relationships can either make us strong in battle or vulnerable to defeat and failure. Any relationship which causes you to

face the devil with a divided attention is a deadly one. A distracted soldier makes himself and his whole army susceptible to defeat. You must consider every relationship you have on the basis of whether it makes you strong and ready to face the enemy, or makes you weak and vulnerable. Every sinful relationship will make you vulnerable to defeat and <u>woeful failure.</u>

"Is any man afraid or faint hearted? ... let him go home so that his brothers will not become disheartened too"

We talked about fear and discouragement as two setbacks to living victoriously. From these words we see that fear is dangerously contagious. Fear in one aspect of your life soon spreads its tentacles into other areas, if not immediately dealt with.

"Is any man afraid or fainthearted?"

This means it does not matter whether that one is a commander of thousands, of hundreds, of fifties or of tens, it does not matter whether he is just an ordinary soldier combatant or non-combatant. As long as you are fainthearted you should better go home. Thus, no matter how significant or insignificant, strong or weak an area of your life is, if you allow fear of any degree to take its hold there, be sure that shall spread like a cancerous cell to other areas of your life.

For some, it may be the fear of responsibility. For others it may be the fear of commitment. Still for some it is just the fear of the uncertain. May I say again that fear is dangerously contagious and must be dealt away with as soon as it is identified or shows its ugly face in one aspect of your life or the other.

All that has been said in this section can be summarized in one pregnant statement: unless you are ready to sacrifice your all and even die in battle you are not ready for confrontation with satan and his cohorts. If there is anything so precious that you cannot give up for the sake of the cross, then your hands cannot be trained for battle. This is just where many disqualify themselves from the battle. They have not ceased to belong to the Kingdom, but they cannot be counted on by the King as combatants. Heaven's omnipotent weapons are only effective in the hands of those who are wholeheartedly given to the battle. Those who have laid all they know they should on the altar of the gospel and any such thing the Master may demand that it be laid down. Are you willing to lay down your life in your battle against the flesh, the world and demons? If so, then all of heaven's power is available to you, and all of creation will obey your orders as you engage the enemy in battle.

Chapter 8

Set up for victory

"**And when the LORD your God has delivered them over to you and you have defeated them, then you must destroy them totally. Make no treaty with them, and show them no mercy**" (Deuteronomy 7:2).

The secret to consistent victory in this never-ending lifetime battle is to treat the enemies of your inheritance in Christ Jesus without pity or mercy. What are the enemies of your full inheritance in Christ Jesus? Sin, the world, the flesh, the things of the world, satan and his demons. A secret to victorious living is that there should be no compromise between you and any of the enemies. The solution to the flesh is crucifixion. The solution to the world is annihilation. Though you may not be able to annihilate the world you can exterminate the love of the world and the love of the things of the world from your heart. Sin must be ruthlessly uprooted from your heart and where possible from your environment. Do not allow anything to deprive you of your full inheritance. No enemy has the right to share your inheritance with you.

Every enemy in the domain of your inheritance must be engaged in battle and overcome. The enemy with which you compromise today will tomorrow deprive you of your complete inheritance by leading you astray from a wholehearted devotion to your God. Satan knows fully well that Omnipotence cannot be available to those who are halfhearted, and so he seeks to weaken believers and the potential damage they can cause to his kingdom by luring them into compromise.

The Lord God warned the Israelites when He said

" But if you do not drive out the inhabitants of the land, those you allow to remain will become barbs in your eyes and thorns in your sides. They will give you trouble in the land where you will live. [56] And then I will do to you what I plan to do to them" (Numbers 33:55-56).

That sin in your life which you have not dealt with is a mighty weapon in the hands of the enemy against you. That attitude of your flesh which you have not put to death is a mighty weapon in the hands of the devil. That love of the world and the things of the world which you have not dealt with is a weapon you are handing the enemy to slay you with. Satan understands spiritual principles and so he seeks to get us into a situation where those laws which govern the conflict will work against us (v56). It is true that God will never be against His children, but the laws He established to govern this universe which cannot be violated will be set in motion against that one that violates them. Once the world, the flesh, and sin are dealt with, satan and his demons have no possibility to inflict damage.

Being careful
"Be careful, or you will be enticed to turn away and worship other gods and bow down to them. Then the anger of the Lord will burn against you..." (Deuteronomy 11:16-17a).

In this lifetime battle of ours, the Lord expects you and I to exercise care and caution in the way we live and interact. He expects us to take necessary preventive measures, being observant and watchful. He expects us to draw lines and respect those lines. Why? Because satan seeks ever to weaken us and make us vulnerable through the subtleness of sin, the flesh and the world.

To be enticed means to be seduced. It means to be deceived and dragged into something in a subtle manner. It means to be led into something without you realizing when and how it happened. To maintain a victor's disposition, you must be careful with your relationships. You must be careful how you interact. You must be careful of who you allow into your spiritual environment. You must be careful from who you receive gifts and free services. You must be careful to whom you show care and concern. Any of the above may lead you into the worship of the god of mammon, the god of sex, the god of fashion, and the god of fame and power.

You must accept people, things, offers, opportunities, and ideas on the basis of whether they will lead you closer God and His plans for your life or away from Him and His plans for your life. Anything or person which draws your thoughts away from God must be rejected. Anything or person which draws your heart away from God must be judged and rejected. Anything which draws you away from a wholehearted devotion and service to God must be rejected.

I want you to understand that there are some offers which are just tests from God. There are some opportunities which are just tests from God. They come to test your commitment and consecration. Do not make yourself an opportunist who just gets into anything, or accepts anything because of the possibilities therein. You must weigh them in light of their eternal values.

From Deuteronomy 13:1-5, we see that the sentence on anybody or anything which seeks to lure your focus away from God is the death penalty. That thing or individual should cease to exist as far as your world is concerned. Count it dead no matter how dear, close, and precious that thing or person may be to you. Show no pity whatsoever in rendering it non-existent in your world. This does not imply physically harming the thing or person, but that you remove it from your heart. Part with it the furthest distance possible. For this is a matter of life or death, success or failure, victory or defeat.

Power in purity
"When you are encamped against your enemies, keep away from everything impure"(Deuteronomy 23:9).

We said earlier that the Christian life is one of continuous warfare. Thus, ours is a permanent encampment against multiple enemies with several routes of attack; sin, the world, the things of the world, the flesh, demons, satan, poverty, sickness etc. To maintain a victor's disposition, there must be moral and physical purity. Purity has power, or better still, purity is power! Physical and moral impurity, especially, makes a soldier at war vulnerable to defeat as this weakens your spiritual defense mechanism and reduces the potentials of your weapons.

Purity compels heaven to align with you in battle!

Purity compels nature to respond to your calls and obey your orders!

Purity provides a habitation for God!

There are impurities of the body, impurities of the soul, and impurities of the spirit. You will do well to keep away from all that can obviously contaminate you. It is written,

> **"Since we have these promises, dear friends, let us purify ourselves from everything that contaminates body and spirit, perfecting holiness out of reverence for God" (2Corinthians 7:1).**

> **"And the very God of peace sanctify you wholly; and I pray God your whole spirit and soul and body be preserved blameless unto the coming of our Lord Jesus Christ" (1Thessalonians 5:23, KJV).**

Satan knows there is power in purity

When Israel came out of Egypt, the king of Moab called for Balaam to place a curse on the Israelites so he could engage them in battle and defeat them. The prophecies of Balaam during this event reveal tremendous truths concerning spiritual warfare. Let us pay careful attention to some verses concerning the matter we are now looking at.

> **"From the rocky peaks I see them, from the heights I view them. I see a people who live apart and do not consider themselves one of the nations" (Numbers 23:9).**

The first lesson we can learn from here about purity is that it begins with the attitude. You must see yourself as one who has been set apart from the world, set apart by God. Unless you have this attitude, you will not be able to keep yourself from those things which contaminate.

When you see yourself as set apart you will not give in to just any pressure from the world to squeeze into its mold. The nations were involved in all kinds of lewdness and acts which defile the body, soul, and spirit. For Israel to remain pure he had to see himself different from the nations; their passions, values, ways and actions.

The second lesson here is this:

"He hath not beheld iniquity in Jacob, neither hath he seen perverseness in Israel: the Lord his God is with him, and the shout of a king is among them"(Numbers 23:21,KJV).

When God does not behold iniquity in your life, when you keep anything of perverse nature far from your life, the result is that God will be with you. And when God is with you, His shout of victory will obviously be heard in your life. Purity makes you strong in battle because God takes side with the pure in heart.

Because God does not find iniquity in Israel, no sorcery, enchantment, divination, incantation, or omen done against him will succeed. Today the number of people actively involved in witchcraft and other satanic practices is rapidly increasing. These ones seek to weaken believers through any means possible.

However, just as it was with Israel so will it be with you, no matter how many thousands of demons are released through those spells and incantations. Let a million demons be released against you, the shield of purity around you will put them to flight for **"righteousness guards the**

man of integrity" (Proverbs 13:6). If you must live beyond the reach of satan and his demons and human agents, live a pure life.

> **"Behold, the people shall rise up as a great lion, and lift up himself as a young lion: he shall not lie down until he eat of the prey, and drink the blood of the slain" (Numbers 23:24, KJV).**

That is the kind of power available to the pure, the power of a lioness, and the power of a wild ox. Remember that, because Moab knew as long as Israel kept himself pure any attempt to engage them in battle will be failure and defeat, through the advice of Balaam, they resorted to seduce Israel into idol worship and sexual immorality. This broke down their wall of defense, incapacitated them and set the laws of spiritual conflict against Israel.

Satan is afraid to attack any child of God, and so he can only appeal through the flesh to lead you into a position where the laws of nature and spiritual conflict begin to work against you. This is the only time he can have an upper hand especially when you fail to quickly acknowledge your sin and repent from it. That is the more reason you must labor not to indulge in sin. Immediately you find yourself in a mess, repent and cut the ground from beneath the enemy so he will have no grounds for accusation.

Keep in phase with the Spirit
For you to maintain a victor's disposition in this conflict against multiple foes with multiple avenues of assault, you've got to keep in step with the Holy Spirit. This is all important and determines whether you meet defeat or victory in the battles of life. I have personally experienced several

defeats when I fail to respond to the voice of the Holy Spirit within. His leading is your only guarantee of victory.

> **"Remember what the Amalekites did to you along the way when you came out of Egypt. [18] When you were weary and worn out, they met you on your journey and cut off all who were lagging behind; they had no fear of God. [19] When the LORD your God gives you rest from all the enemies around you in the land he is giving you to possess as an inheritance, you shall blot out the memory of Amalek from under heaven. Do not forget!"**
> **(Deuteronomy 25:17-19)**

To lag behind is to be out of phase with the Holy Spirit. When a man is out of step with the Holy Spirit he may either be lagging behind or may have rushed ahead of the Holy Spirit. Both situations are dangerous and make you vulnerable to defeat. Moments of spiritual, physical or moral weariness are very vulnerable moments. That is when Amalek strikes easiest and hardest.

Amalek is anything that stands on your way to a victorious life, anything that seeks to prevent you from entering into the fullness of your inheritance. If ever you must be watchful, it is when you feel weary in any area of your life. Such moments of challenge should push you to cling more to the Holy Spirit. The temptation during such times of weariness is for the line of communication with Heaven to be interrupted.

If you must keep in step with the Holy Spirit, there must be a commitment to act when God wants you to act, where He wants you to act, and how He wants you to act. When you fail to, or refuse to, act when God gives you the opportunity, that window may be closed for a very long time or even permanently closed. He may expect you to act even when there is the fiercest opposition there can ever be in a situation, when the difficulties and impossibilities are most evident.

May I say it again that there are moments when a window of Sprit engineered opportunity closes if not made use of. This is the more reason why you must be committed to move according the dictates of the Holy Sprit and not of the flesh.

Weapons with God's backing will accomplish much, but those same weapons without His backing will amount to nothing. Gifts with the anointing of God will accomplish the extraordinary, but those same gifts without His anointing will amount to naught. Talents with the anointing will produce overwhelming results, but those same talents in the power of the flesh will hinder the work of God. And God's anointing is only available when He leads.

Every capacity, capability or ability will produce meaningful results only through God. There is no greater arrogance and presumption than to go into something knowing fully well that God is not going with you. There is no greater folly than to face the enemy no matter how small in the power of your corrupt flesh. The greatest favor you can do yourself in moments of uncertainty is to wait for His presence and precedence. What makes the difference is not the nature or magnitude of your weapons, zeal and determination, but God's accompanying presence. Do not afford to make the same mistake the Israelites once made:

"Then you replied, "We have sinned against the LORD. We will go up and fight, as the LORD our God commanded us." So every one of you put on his weapons, thinking it easy to go up into the hill country.

But the LORD said to me, "Tell them, `Do not go up and fight, because I will not be with you. You will be defeated by your enemies.' So I told you, but you would not listen. You rebelled against the LORD's command and in your arrogance you marched up into the hill country. 44 The Amorites who lived in those hills came out against you; they chased you like a swarm of bees and beat you down from Seir all the way to Hormah. 45 You came back and wept before the LORD, but he paid no attention to your weeping and turned a deaf ear to you. 46 And so you stayed in Kadesh many days--all the time you spent there" (Deuteronomy 1:41-46)

Be on the offensive

What we are going to say here will be based on the eighteenth psalm. We shall cite only the verses we need here, but it will do you good to read the entire psalm.

From Egypt to Canaan, the Israelites were always on the offensive against their enemies. The fact that we must be in phase with the Holy Spirit does not mean you will just fold your arms and do nothing. The Holy Spirit will not tell you to do the things you already know you should do, that is, do not expect to be led to pray before you pray.

Do not expect to be led to witness before you witness. It is true that there are moments when He will prompt you to pray for a particular situation or witness to a particular person, but this is not the rule. You must be on the lookout for possible enemy targets to confront with the Holy Spirit power under His leading. You will have to take the offensive, all what you need is the guarantee of God's presence and backing.

Once you confront a situation and you have the green light of His backing go ahead, He will restrain you when and if need be.

Like the Psalmist who said, **"With your help I can advance against a troop; with my God I can scale a wall" (Psalm 18:29),** daily you must solicit and appropriate the presence and companionship to be able to overcome all the barriers of the enemy as you lunch your offence against him.

To attack a troop means you going into the enemy camp, scaling any walls of defense, storming the prison yards and setting free captives. It is time to move from the defensive to the offensive.

How to appropriate the victory

"I pursued my enemies and overtook them; I did not turn back till they were destroyed. I crushed them so that they could not rise; they fell beneath my feet" (Psalm 18:37-38).

1. be on the offensive:

"I pursued my enemies…" you must be on the offensive against sin, the flesh, sickness, the world, demons and all that has to do with the enemy first in your life then in your environment. Sin must be pursued out of your life; sickness must to expelled, the world must be exterminated from your heart, and demons cast out. Then will you be able to confront the enemy in your environment.

2. Give in your all:

"I did not turn back till they were destroyed". You must enter every battle not to withdraw until the enemy has not only been overtaken but totally destroyed. Once you give yourself any possibility of turning back before the enemy is overtaken and destroyed, victory cannot be won. So, put on the attitude not only of persisting but to also prevail – victory or no turning back!

3. Go in for complete annihilation:

"I crushed them so that they could not rise." Victory is not assured over that particular enemy until there is absolutely no possibility for the enemy to rise again. The enemy defeated but not annihilated will regain strength and rise again to confront you, this time around with a much stronger resistance. Thus, in dealing with sin, the world or the flesh, deal with them from the roots, uprooting and burning every trace in your life.

chapter 9

Your counter strategy

How can we maintain our God –given victory? How can we continue to fight from a position of victory? This chapter is meant just for that. Not how we can gain the victory, but how we can keep and continue to keep the victory. Below are strategies to help you maintain victory:

1). **Innocence about evil**:

The Lord Jesus in sending out His disciples told them to be **"as innocent as doves" (Matthew 10:16).** What should they be innocent about? We find the answer in Romans. The Apostle Paul wrote to the Romans saying, **"But I want you to be wise about what is good and innocent about what is evil" (Romans 16:19).** Labor to be innocent concerning evil. This means you should do everything to avoid learning evil. Avoid watching movies or going places or keeping the company of people that will expose you to the knowledge of evil.

To be innocent as used here means three categories of things:

i). not tainted with sin; blameless, pure; ignorant of evil.

ii). Free from qualities that can harm or injure

iii). Lacking in worldly knowledge.

This is how the savior wants us to be. Knowledge of evil does not give you victory over evil but instead makes you vulnerable. The original intentions of God were tied to man's innocence of evil, but as soon as man became aware of the possibility of evil his heart became inclined towards evil all the time.

2). **Self-control:**

"Be self-controlled…" (1 Peter 5:8)

Self-control is defined as the act, power or habit of having one's faculties or energies under the control of the will (Funk and Wagnals). Here, faculties refer to any mode of bodily or mental behavior as implying a natural endowment or acquired power e.g. Seeing, feeling, reasoning etc.

You need to control the things you see, listen to, and think about or imagine. You need to have mastery over your feelings. You need to control your speech. I want you to understand that to keep your victory you must exercise self-control.

Some facts about self-control
<u>it is for all believers:</u>
> **"Teach the older men to be temperate, worthy of respect, self-controlled, and sound in faith, in love and in endurance. Likewise, teach the older women to be reverent in the way they live, not to be**

slanderers or addicted to much wine, but to teach what is good. **4 Then they can train the younger women to love their husbands and children, 5 to be self-controlled and pure, to be busy at home, to be kind, and to be subject to their husbands, so that no one will malign the word of God. Similarly, encourage the young men to be self-controlled" (Titus 2:2-6).**

From the above passage we see that believers, irrespective of their age or sex are commanded to exercise self-control. The command is for older men, older women, younger men and younger women.

it is indispensable for leadership:

"Now the overseer must be above reproach, the husband of but one wife, temperate, self-controlled, respectable, hospitable, able to teach" (1Timothy 3:2).

"Rather he must be hospitable, one who loves what is good, who is self-controlled, upright, holy and disciplined" (Titus 1:8).

Self-control is indispensable for anyone aspiring to Christian leadership. You need to have yourself under control to help others acquire self-control and keep things under control.

lack of self-control makes you vulnerable:

"Like a city whose walls are broken down is a man who lacks self-control" (Proverbs 25:28).

"Do not deprive each other except by mutual consent and for a time, so that you may devote yourselves to prayer. Then come together again so that Satan will not tempt you because of your lack of self-control" (1 Corithians 7:5).

In ancient times, a city's strength was measured by the strength of it's walls. One without any wall was vulnerable to attack by any invading forces. Here, the Bible likens self-control to the walls of a city. It tells you that without self control you and I become totally vulnerable to the attacks of satan. Do you lack self-control? Then you are totally vulnerable to defeat. Lack of it exposes you to the temptations of the flesh and the devil.

it prepares you for action:
> **"The end of all things is near. Therefore be clear minded and self-controlled so that you can pray" (1 Peter 4:7).**
>
> **"Therefore, prepare your minds for action; be self-controlled; set your hope fully on the grace to be given you when Jesus Christ is revealed" (1Peter 1:13).**

When we are self-controlled, we can pray, we are prepared for action, ready to move with the Spirit of God.

How to acquire self-control
The Bible instructs us to **"For this very reason, make every effort to add to your faith goodness; and to goodness, knowledge; ⁶ and to knowledge, self-control; and to self-control, perseverance; and to perseverance, godliness; ⁷ and to godliness, brotherly kindness; and to brotherly kindness, love" (2Peter 1:5-7).**

Now, you see the position self-control occupies in that tree of virtues. Without it there is no way the other virtues can be added. However, though it is indispensable, it is not available in the market for you and I to go purchase. It is a part of the fruit of the Sprit (Galatians

5:23). As we ensure to live a Spirit-filled life, we will be able to exercise self-control.

3). **Alertness**

"So then, let us not be like others, who are asleep, but let us be alert and self-controlled" (1 Thessalonians 5:6).

"Be on your guard…" (1Corinthians 16:13).

To keep your victory, you must be keenly watchful, be on the lookout and be ready for sudden action. You must be watchful against the influence of the world upon you, against the wiles and schemes of satan. Never be involved in anything that renders you unfit for sudden action or impedes your ability and disposition to be watchful and vigilant. The question we must all ask ourselves at a time as this is "what are the things which can make me to lose my vigilant disposition?"

Let's turn back to the Book to examine some of such things:

"Come, all you beasts of the field, come and devour, all you beasts of the forest! Israel's watchmen are blind, they all lack knowledge; they are all mute dogs, they cannot bark; they lie around and dream, they love to sleep. They are dogs with mighty appetites; they never have enough. They are shepherds who lack understanding; they all turn to their own way, each seeks his own gain. "Come," each one cries, "let me get wine! Let us drink our fill of beer! And tomorrow will be like today, or even far better" (Isaiah 56:9-12).

What do the beasts of the field represent? Enemies of God's flock, His people! They have an invitation to devour and cause havoc when the watchmen-those called to be vigilant:

 -are blind

-Lack knowledge

-Cannot bark

First, the job of the watchman is to see danger coming and warn the people. His duty is to stand in the gap between the danger and the people. Hence, if the watchmen are blind danger would come unnoticed and reach the people without prior notice.

Second, the job of the watchman is to know the state of affairs –the things which are happening in the midst of the people he is called to watch over. This knowledge guides him on how to pray and when it is lacking, the watchman cannot be effective. The barking of the watchman is meant to keep away intruders and trespassers. It is a signal to the people that there's something strange in the environment. When watchmen cannot bark, intruders go around freely and unhindered without any fear of alarm. Why do the watchmen fail? Why are they blind? Why can't they bark?

i.   *They lie around and dream:*

This talks of nothing but ease and absentmindedness. They are not conscious of their responsibility and so they can only daydream. Any lover of ease and anyone who lacks focus cannot be watchful.

ii. *They love to sleep:*

Laziness and love of sleep is another cause of failure to watch. If one who is called to stay awake and be alert loves to sleep, then he can't succeed in keeping guard. There is one such man who decided to go to sleep in the midst of war (king Saul, see 1 Samuel 26). Instead of being watchful he went to sleep and for sure his enemy, **"David took the spear and water jug near Saul's head, and they left" (1Samuel 26:12).** Have you been stripped of your weapon and sustenance because of love of sleep? Are you like Saul, at the mercy of your enemy? For how long shall you continue in your slumber? There is an English saying that "let the sleeping dog lie" but the Bible says, **"Wake up o sleeper and rise from the dead"** (Ephesians 5:14).

iii. *They have mighty appetites:*

This is nothing but the love of food. No one who is a lover of food can successfully keep watch. Love of food is a resignation from alertness and watchfulness.

iv. *They never have enough:*

The one who lacks contentment would run even after the offers of the enemy. The watchdog which is not satisfied with what its master offers it will be distracted with what the enemy throws at it in order to have access while it occupies itself. Lack of contentment is the cause of the defeat and ruin of so many lives. If I may ask you a question, are you contented? Do you have the rare jewel of Christian contentment or you are one of those who crave for more and more without restraint?

v. *They lack understanding*:

We all need to understand the times we are living in order to be alert. We need to understand the events which are happening. Lack of this understanding will cause us to fail to be alert.

vi. *They all turn to their own ways:*

Do you remember that famous passage in Isaiah 53? **"We all, like sheep have gone astray, each of us to his own way…"** (v6). When we turn to our own ways, to do the things we've chosen for ourselves, we lose the capacity to be alert, ready for action. There's no greater deception than a man following his own ways and yet thinks he is still on the right path, meanwhile he is as far from where God wants him to be as the east is from the west.

vii.   *Each seeks his own gain:*

We are called to "seek first His Kingdom and His righteousness". When we run after personal gain, we take our focus off from Him to ourselves and the things we are running after. I am afraid that as the believers of the early church allowed the devil to creep too fast into the church, the modern church is doing that at an alarming rate because **"everyone looks out for his own interests and not those of Jesus Christ" (Philippians 2:21).**

Everyone seems to be looking out for personal gain and the church seems to be in a rift without any disposition to guard her conquered territory. Are you watchful to see that the interests of Christ through the cross are sought and nothing else? If not, then, you can not be truly alert.

viii.   Love of pleasure (v 12):

The lover of pleasure cannot be watchful. Nothing saps away spiritual energy and the capacity to keep watch like pleasure does. Do you want to be alert? Then keep away from the love of pleasure and frivolity. Do not be given over to a life that seeks to find its satisfaction in pleasure. Prayer is one way to exercise alertness; **"And pray in the Spirit on all occasions with all kinds of prayers and requests. With this in mind, be alert and always keep on praying for all the saints"(Ephesians 6:18).**

We must pray and keep praying to maintain our conquered territory. We must also be alert towards the coming of the King, **"No one knows about that day or hour, not even the angels in heaven, nor the Son, but only the Father. ^{33} Be on guard! Be alert"! You do not know when that time will come" (Mark 13:32-33).** Living in the consciousness of His eminent return will help you to stay awake and alert, prepared to meet Him. Know that your Master is coming again, and that He is coming soon.

4`). **Resisting the devil**

> **"Submit yourselves, then, to God. Resist the devil, and he will flee from you" (James 4:7).**
>
> **"Resist him, standing firm in the faith, because you know that your brothers throughout the world are undergoing the same kind of sufferings'(1 Peter 5:9).**

We have been commanded to resist the devil, meaning we have to act counter to, for the purpose of stopping, preventing, and defeating the activities and plans of satan. The Greek word used in both verses above is "anthistemi" which is a composition of two other Greek words: "anti" which means contrast and "histemi" which means to stand. (see 436, 473 and 2476 of the Greek dictionary in Strong's exhaustive concordance). Thus, it talks of active opposition to the devil. In the next chapter, let's discuss some strategies to resist the devil.

Chapter 10

Your Counter Strategy 2

How to resist the devil

i. Through knowledge of God:

"With flattery he will corrupt those who have violated the covenant, but the people who know their God will firmly resist him" (Daniel 11:32).

There are times when the devil can only use flattery and subtlety to gain grounds. The only people who will be able to resist him are those who know their God. The Hebrew word used for "know" here is "yada", which is the same word used to describe sexual relationship between a man and a woman.(3045, Strong's Hebrew dictionary). Thus, the "know" here is not a mental knowledge but that of real intimacy with God. This is the kind of knowledge that gives firm resistance to the flattery and deception of satan.

It is the same word used in Jeremiah 9:24. God delights in us knowing Him as one who expresses kindness, justice and righteousness. His kindness includes His mercies, compassion, tenderheartedness, goodness etc. He wants us to know Him as One who seeks what is best for us. He wants us to know that He is not an austere God, a ruthless taskmaster. This would help you resist the lies of the devil which may suggest that God does not love you nor does He care about your welfare.

Knowing Him in His justice will cause you to understand that He will never violate His principles of justice as revealed in His eternal Word. It lets you to know that every word of His that spells out His judgment on sin will come to pass. It will cause you to know that anyone who continues in sin will reap the consequence of eternal damnation. This will keep you from believing the lies of the enemy which say that God is so kind and generous to send anyone to hell. Know Him in His righteousness, that all what He does is righteous, that He is a God in whom is no sin or wrongdoing. Know your God!

ii. *Through submission to God*:

"Submit yourselves, then, to God. Resist the devil, and he will flee from you. (James 4:7).

As you give yourself humbly to God in submission to His plans and workings in your life, you are opposing satan's plans for you and therefore resisting him.

iii. *Through intimacy with God:*

"Come near to God and He will come near to you" (James 4:8a).

Drawing near to God signifies getting close and intimate to Him.

iv. *Through purity of heart:*

> "Wash your hands, you sinners, and purify your hearts, you who are double-minded" (James 4:8b).

Remember we said the devil's primary job is to accuse us before the Father. As we purify our hearts and live pure lives, we cut the ground from beneath his feet, thereby resisting him i.e. actively opposing him.

5. Standing firm in your faith

> "Resist him, standing firm in the faith, because you know that your brothers throughout the world are undergoing the same kind of sufferings"(1 Peter 5:9).
>
> "Therefore, my dear brothers, stand firm. Let nothing move you. Always give yourselves fully to the work of the Lord, because you know that your labor in the Lord is not in vain" (1 Corinthians 15:58).
>
> "Be on your guard; stand firm in the faith; be men of courage; be strong" (1 C0rinthians 16:13).

To stand firm and be moved by nothing requires strength and courage. We must allow the Spirit to fill us each day and inspire us to be bold like He did the apostles of old. If there is one thing you should be aware of, it is that standing firm is not an option but a must. It is written that, "if you do not stand firm in your faith, you will not stand at all." (Isaiah 7:9b). So, it is either you are standing firm or you are not standing! No midway between.

Are you standing firm? It is a must if you have to continue to stand against (resist) the work of satan.

Why you should stand firm

> "Do not be afraid. Stand firm and you will see the deliverance the LORD will bring you today. The Egyptians you see today you will never see again" (Exodus 14:13).
>
> "You will not have to fight this battle. Take up your positions; stand firm and see the deliverance the LORD will give you, O Judah and Jerusalem. Do not be afraid; do not be discouraged. Go out to face them tomorrow, and the LORD will be with you" (2Chronicles 20:17).

Like I said before, standing firm requires certain virtues: lack of fear, courage, and strength.

It will mean confronting the enemy when need be. And in doing that deliverance is sure to come. Will you confront the enemy's stronghold in your life? Will you gather courage and obtain your deliverance?

- standing firm brings great victory

> "*10 but he stood his ground* and struck down the Philistines till his hand grew tired and froze to the sword. The LORD brought about a great victory that day ... 12 But Shammah *took his stand* in the middle of the field. He defended it and struck the Philistines down, and the LORD brought about a great victory" (2 Samuel 23:9-12).

The church today needs Eleazars and Shammahs, men and women who will stand their ground when every other person is retreating. The church needs stouthearted men and women who will stand their ground in the midst of every battle to preserve already conquered territory for God, to give daily victory over the invading forces of hell.

How to stand firm

i. *Making up your mind:*

"Stand firm, then, and do not let yourself be burdened again by a yoke of slavery" (Galatians 5:1).

You've got to make up your mind to stand firm and no let yourself be carried away by any deception of the enemy. "Do not let…" means it is in your power to continue to stand firm or to give up. Stand on God's promises (Word): **"He lifted me out of the slimy pit, out of the mud and mire; he set my feet on a rock and gave me a firm place to stand." (Psalm 40:2).** What is this firm place to stand on? God's word! Every other thing you stand on will be slime and mire. The only sure place to stand and stand firm is the written and spoken word of God. Do you want to stand firm? Then stand on the promises of God and on them only. The possibility of anyone to stand firm lies on the kind of place or surface he is standing on. Every effort to stand firm on slime or mire will be a waste of time.

ii. *Hold on to what you know:*

"So then, brothers, stand firm and hold to the teachings we passed on to you, whether by word of mouth or by letter" (2Thessalonians 2:15).

To stand firm you must hold on to truth and sound doctrine taught. By rejecting any truth revealed is to begin to drift away. It is written somewhere, **"we must pay more careful attention, therefore, to what we have heard, so that we do not drift away" (Hebrews 2:1).** Rejecting Bible truths is to reject the anchor to which your boat should be tied for it to be secured. Hold on to the truth you know. It is not an option but a must, "we must pay…" does that sound liking doing it when you feel like?

iii. *Be patient:*

"You too, be patient and stand firm, because the Lord's coming is near" (James 5:8) .

You must be patient with yourself, be patient with others and be patient with God. Give God time to work in you and to fulfill His word in your life. Many people fall because at some point in time, they become impatient with God and begin to doubt the very words of God and even their own salvation. This gives the devil grounds to inflict more doubt into their hearts and the outcome is that, the truths they once knew and believed are abandoned. You must be patient.

iv. Put on God's armor:

(see Ephesians 6:11-17)

Every part of this armor is important, leaving any one part out is to make yourself vulnerable to defeat. Ensure that where duty calls, anytime it calls, you are not found wanting in any part.

6). Have a forgiving heart

> **"If you forgive anyone, I also forgive him. And what I have forgiven--if there was anything to forgive--I have forgiven in the sight of Christ for your sake, [11] in order that Satan might not outwit us. For we are not unaware of his schemes" (2 Corinthians 2:10-11).**

When unforgiveness is kept in the heart in whatever degree, it gives satan grounds to employ his wiles and schemes. Why? Because unforgiveness will give birth to hatred and eventually vengeance will follow. Unforgiveness will also give birth to anger and the presence of anger in the heart gives the devil a foothold.

7). **Use the blood:**
"They overcame him by the blood of the Lamb…" (Revelations 12:11).

We can effectively use the blood of the Lamb only when we are alert, standing firm, self-controlled and resisting the devil. There are many people who try to use the blood when they are not standing firm in their faith nor do they live up to Bible standards. This can be nothing but deception and they soon find, for them, it does not work. To use the blood, you must be in right standing with God.

8). **Use the word:**

When the devil launched his attack on the Lord in the wilderness, our Lord used the word to defeat him. You too can use the word to defeat the enemy. Speak out the word of God to him when he attacks. It is a mighty weapon.

Also, the Bible says, **"they overcame him by the blood of the Lamb and by the word of their testimony" (Revelations 12:11)**. Declaring and proclaiming God's goodness to you, counting your blessings and naming them will put the enemy to flight. You can use all of the above to counter your enemy and maintain your God-given victory.

Chapter 11

Slaying the monster

(dealing with the greatest limitation)

Y ou might be wondering what this thing of a monster is. For some, their minds have quickly turned to the devil, thinking he is the monster that must be slain. Well, he can only be slain by God Himself and the time is soon coming when he and his activities will be hurled into the lake of fire and put to a permanent end.

The monster I am referring to is that thing called sin. Nothing brings limitation to the believer's potentials like sin does. In slaying this monster you will be dealing with the greatest limitation that has plagued humankind, which can ever confront you. And in doing this all other limitations will be weaken permanently.

The plain truth is that, too many of us have a very shallow understanding of what sin is, its effects and damages. This is seen in the way even professing Christians deal with sin in its different manifestations in their everyday living.

This teaching is designed to bring out to us a deeper understanding of what the Bible teaches about sin, not for some mental knowledge, but for knowledge that will affect the heart and bring freedom in the spirit leading to spiritual fulfillment.

Its manifestations (what sin is)

"Sin" appears to be a very general term as used in the Bible. There are principally four words used in the Bible, in both the old and New Testaments to mean, "sin". They are: sin, transgression, trespass, and iniquity.

We shall examine each of these in the various forms in which they are used in both Testaments so that by the end of this study we will be able to know when, how and why sin is committed and when, how and why sin is confessed.

Sin

There are a number of Hebrew and Greek words used in the Bible, which are translated as "sin" in our English Bibles. We shall examine some of them that will help us in our study:

- Ashâm: this is translated as "a fault". In our English language a fault can mean a slight offense, failure or negligence. Thus, neglect for, or failure to carry out our Christian responsibilities towards one another and towards the unsaved is sin in the sight of God. Our neglect for prayer and all that will cause us to grow in our knowledge and service for Him and for mankind is sin. The above word is used also to describe the world's neglect for God (Jeremiah

51:5). Do not look light on your neglect of your duties as a Christian. Proverbs 14:9 says, "Fools mock at sin (ashâm)" (KJV, emphasis mine). Therefore, God expects us to take our failures and negligence just as serious as murder is taken.

- Chêt: this is translated as, "a crime". A crime is any grave offense against morality or social order. It is anything wicked. This refers to both our actions (Hosea 13:12, Ezekiel 3: 21, Jeremiah 32:35) and our words (Ecclesiastes 5:6).
- châttâ'ah: this is translated as " a habitual offense". These are wrongs, which have become like habits in the life of the individual concerned and are therefore regarded as normal. It will include lateness, orgies, gambling etc.
- âvôn which is translated as perversity. Perversity is the state of being perverse-anything which is different or varying from the correct. Homosexuality, lesbianism, pedophilia, masturbation etc. all fall in this category.
- Peshâ, which is translated as "rebellion". Rebellion is resistance to any authority or established usage. When we fail to submit to authority we "peshâ". When we use things for the wrong purpose e.g. using your mouth to curse (Proverbs 10:19), is peshâ.
- Ashmâh, shâgâh: both words refer to the cause of the action rather than the action itself; that which causes a man to trespass, to stray, and to wander. Anything which misleads or deceives or causes to sin through ignorance. All that will cause you to deviate from godly principles fall in this category. All that which competes with God in your life falls in this category, because it causes you not to give God the place he deserves. Now, let us look at some practical

examples: television and entertainment in general become sin when they cause us to miss our focus. Films become sin if they will lead you to deviate from proper behavior and conduct, if they will cause you to harbor ungodly thoughts and motives and desires even for a moment. Relationships or material possessions become sin if and when they mislead us in life. Are your relationships causing you to move closer your God-ordained destiny or away from them?

A number of Greek words used in the New Testament are also translated as "sin":

- ➢ Hamartanō: this means to miss the mark i.e. falling short of the expectations of God as expressed in his laws, ordinances, precepts and principles.
- ➢ Hamartia refers to the sinful nature of man. That which man got not because of his own actions but because of the original fall.
- ➢ Paraptōma: this means a sideslip, lapse or deviation; unintentional error; a fall. All those things you might do which are wrong but were unintentional fall in this category. They are sins that were not planned or premeditated.
- ➢ Parabasis: translated as violation; breaking. These are actions or words, which are intentionally non-compliant with set moral and spiritual laws.

Transgression

Again, we shall just examine some words used in both the Hebrew Old Testament and the Greek New Testament translated as "to transgress" or "transgression".

In the Hebrew Old Testament we have words like:

- Bâgad: this means to act covertly. Anything that is done with the intention of hiding it is sin. For example, a man can make a gift to a woman or vice versa with the intention that no one else should ever know about it, or write a letter of which he wishes nobody knows the content of that letter.
- mâ'al: which means "cover up". These are actions or words one may use to cover up the real motives of something. E.g. a man may make a gift to another with the intent of winning the others favor while he acts as though he were just being generous, or may ask a question with the intent of insinuating or instigating something while he pretends he just wanted to know something.
- ma'al: which means treachery or falsehood. This is closely related to the word described above, denoting all that which is false, but goes further to include acts that violate confidence or allegiance, acts of cheating, fraud and disloyalty.
- ´âbar: meaning to cross over. This describes that which goes beyond prescribed limits e.g. entering a room you are not allowed to, reading someone else's confidential documents. In general getting out of proper bounds.
- Pâshâ: to break away from just authority. This talks of the tendency and acts of independence from any authority over one's life. Refusal to be accountable to anybody is sin. This also includes man's tendency to be independent of God's rule.

Some of the words used in the Greek new Testaments are:
- Anŏmia: illegality; violation of law. E.g. driving a car without a driver's license, driving a car without insurance, overloading,

breaking speed limits etc. are all, illegal and therefore are, regarded as transgressions in the sight of God.
- Parabainō: to go contrary to. There are people with the tendency to always do the contrary to any given instruction. E.g. " no body should come late", such a person will do all to be late even if he had the opportunity to be early, or " let's all fast tomorrow", and such a person will decide to eat. That too is transgression.

Trespass
To trespass means "to violate willfully and forcibly the personal or property rights of another". It also means to pass the bounds of propriety or rectitude.

It has similar meaning to the Hebrew âshâm and peshâ but with the peculiarity of violation of personal rights.

Iniquity
Iniquity means deviation from right; gross injustice; wrong act; unjust thing or deed.

We shall examine words in Both the Testaments to bring out the full meanings of this term.

In the Hebrew Old Testament the following words are used:
- `âven: it means to pant or exert oneself after vanity. This talks of the folly of running after that which the world runs after, of no use or value in eternity but the increase of man's pride of life.
- Havvâh: to eagerly covet; naughtiness. All little disobediences, greed etc. fall in this category.
- Âvâh: to crook; to do amiss.
- Âmâl: worry of mind or body. There is no justifiable reason for the worry of mind or body. This is iniquity in the sight of God.

In the New Testament we have words like "adikēma" which means, "wrong done" and "adikia" which means "injustice". Thus, any wrongdoing is sin and any act of injustice and partiality is sin.

The above detailed descriptions have let us to see what sin is, when sin is committed, how sin is committed, and to an extent, why sin is committed. The next chapter is to let us see the dangers of sin- what sin does to a man.

Chapter 12

The destructive power of sin

What sin does to a man!

Sin is man's greatest limitation:

"Return, O Israel, to the LORD your God. Your sins have been your downfall!" (Hosea 14:1)

A downfall is that which causes a man to flow downward or to aim low. Sin is that which causes a man to operate far below his God-given potentials, as we shall see.

❖ **Sin robs a man of his anointing:**

"Do not cast me from your presence or take your Holy Spirit from me" (Psalm 51:11).

When David sinned, he asked God not to take the Holy Sprit from him. He understood that sin robs a man of his anointing and his right to the Spirit's anointing. About the Lord Jesus, the Father says, **"you have loved righteousness and hated wickedness, therefore God, your God, has set you above your companions by *anointing you* with the oil of**

Joy" **(Hebrews 1:9, emphasis mine)**. Why was He anointed? Because He loved righteousness and hated wickedness. No one practicing or living in any manner of sin has a right to the Spirit's anointing.

- ❖ **Sin robs a man of vision and capacity to see:**

"O my God, I am too ashamed and disgraced to lift up my face to you, my God, because our sins are higher than our heads and our guilt has reached to the heavens" (Ezra 9:6)

If you are sitting in a room, you can only see upward as far as the ceiling of that room. A man can only see as far as that which blocks his view permits him. When a man's sins are higher than his head, then he cannot see further than his sins, but only to the level of his sins. That is why the sinner can only see the now. He or she is concerned only about the pleasures of now, the gains of now, and the satisfaction of now. Sin blocks a man's view of eternity and the eternal and all what he or she can think of is the ephemeral.

- ❖ **Sin incapacitates a man and renders him unproductive or underproductive:**

"if I have raised my hand against the fatherless, knowing that I had influence in court, then let my arm fall from the shoulder, let it be broken off at the joint" (Job 31:21-22).

If a man's arm is dislocated from its joint and broken off his shoulder, is there any greater way to incapacitate a man? A man who is incapacitated becomes unproductive. That is why a sinner has no use in the house of God. Sin will block you from being used of God.

- ❖ **Sin robs a man of his dignity**:

"How the gold has lost its luster, the fine gold become dull! The sacred gems are scattered at the head of every street. How the

precious sons of Zion, once worth their weight in gold, are now considered as pots of clay, the work of a potter's hands!" (Lamentations 4:1-2)

The dignity and glory of any child of God lies in his or her living the life God has called him or her to; living in holiness and apart for God. Israel became worthless because they failed to live as God's own people and began worshipping idols like the heathen. When a child of God begins to live carelessly like the heathen do, he or she loses his or her worth in the sight of God.

❖ **Sin deprives a man of God's favor:**

"But your iniquities have separated you from your God; your sins have hidden his face from you, so that he will not hear" (Isaiah 59:2).

"Then they will cry out to the LORD, but he will not answer them. At that time he will hide his face from them because of the evil they have done" (Micah 3:4).

God's face and hand represent His blessings and His favor. What greater woe is there than for a man to cry out with no God to help him in time of need? God says in His word, "call upon me in the day of trouble; I will deliver you…" (Psalm 50:15), but sin will keep Him from fulfilling that promise in your life.

❖ **Sin exalts a man's enemies above him:**

"But they forgot the LORD their God; so he sold them into the hand of Sisera, the commander of the army of Hazor, and into the hands of the Philistines and the king of Moab, who fought against them. [10] They cried out to the LORD and said, `We have sinned; we have forsaken the LORD and served the Baals and the

Ashtoreths. But now deliver us from the hands of our enemies, and we will serve you.' ¹¹ Then the LORD sent Jerub-Baal, Barak, Jephthah and Samuel, and he delivered you from the hands of your enemies on every side, so that you lived securely" (1Samuel 12:9-10).

"Israel has sinned; they have violated my covenant, which I commanded them to keep. They have taken some of the devoted things; they have stolen, they have lied, they have put them with their own possessions. ¹² That is why the Israelites cannot stand against their enemies; they turn their backs and run because they have been made liable to destruction. I will not be with you anymore unless you destroy whatever among you is devoted to destruction" (Joshua 7:11-12).

Once there is sin in your life, you can't stand up against the evil one and his hosts, because the sin in your life gives them an upper hand over you. Why? Because the power of the cross can never be made manifest through a life that loves and cherishes sin.

❖ **Sin disqualifies a man from God's presence:**

"So the LORD God banished him from the Garden of Eden to work the ground from which he had been taken" (Genesis 3:23)

(see also Psalm 15 & Psalm 24: 3-6).

God is most holy, and there is nothing celebrated by all creation like His holiness. The proclamation of His holiness seems to be the anthem of Heaven sung continually without ceasing. Because of His holiness, He cannot tolerate sin in His presence. The infinitely holy God cannot come in contact with sin. The only time He did that was in the person of His Son when He bore the sins of the whole world on dark Calvary. Even then, He had to turn His face from He who carried the sins of the world. The intensity of God's holiness will destroy whatever carries sin when He makes His presence manifest. It is for this reason God will not manifest His presence where sin is present. Do you want to have access into His manifest presence? Lead a holy life, steering clear of sin.

❖ **Sin makes a man a physical and spiritual vagabond:**
"Today you are driving me from the land, and I will be hidden from your presence; I will be a restless wanderer on the earth, and whoever finds me will kill me" (Genesis 4:14).

"All of us have become like one who is unclean, and all our righteous acts are like filthy rags; we all shrivel up like a leaf, and like the wind our sins sweep us away" (Isaiah 64:6).

Until Cain sinned against God, he had somewhere to call home. When he sinned even after God had forewarned him to guard against sin, he was banished from the presence of God and from that time on he became a vagabond. All he could do was wander from place to place.

To the believer, there's no shelter, no home, but the presence of God and if you cannot dwell in His presence, certainly there is no place you can call home. For how long shall you continue to wander? Is it not time for you to return home? Sin reduces a man to nothing. Living in sin makes you like autumn leaves which are blown and tossed by the wind, without any direction, will or purpose. Wherever the wind blows that's where it goes. Sin makes a man to lose his purpose in life.

❖ **Sin make a man vulnerable:**
- *To disease*

> "But the LORD inflicted serious diseases on Pharaoh and his household because of Abram's wife Sarai." (Genesis 12:17)

Sin exposes you to sickness and disease. The greater part of diseases and sicknesses are caused and transmitted by sin. Do you recall, in the Gospels, when the Lord healed some people He emphasized that they should go and sin no more? Because He understood that sin makes a man vulnerable to disease.

- *to curses,*

> "Therefore the LORD, the God of Israel, declares: `I promised that your house and your father's house would minister before me forever.' But now the LORD declares: `Far be it from me! Those who honor me I will honor, but those who despise me will be disdained. ^{31} The time is coming when I will cut short your strength and the strength of your father's house, so that there will not be an old man in your family line ^{32} and you will see distress in my dwelling. Although good will be done to Israel, in your family line there will never be an old man. ^{33} Every one of you that I do not cut off from my altar will be spared only to blind your eyes with tears and to grieve your heart, and all your descendants will die in the prime of life." (1Samuel 2:31-33) (see also 2samuel 12:9-10).

Sin makes a man vulnerable to curses. The sad thing about curses is that often it goes beyond the individual concerned to his posterity. Why should you make your descendants suffer because of some indulgence of yours? Keep away from sin; it has no pleasant reward for you or your descendants.

❖ **Sin blinds a man to God's justice and holiness:**

> "For the grace of God that brings salvation has appeared to all men. ¹² It teaches us to say "No" to ungodliness and worldly passions, and to live self-controlled, upright and godly lives in this present age" (Titus 2:11-12).

> "If we deliberately keep on sinning after we have received the knowledge of the truth, no sacrifice for sins is left, ²⁷ but only a fearful expectation of judgment and of raging fire that will consume the enemies of God. ²⁸ Anyone who rejected the law of Moses died without mercy on the testimony of two or three witnesses" (Hebrew 10:26-29).

I have often heard people try to exalt the grace of God above His holiness. It is true that the grace of God is infinite, but to assume that it is available for you each time you sin even deliberately is to be presumptuous. I wonder if many have read the above verses in scripture! The passage from Titus lets us know that the grace of God has the following qualities:

- i) it has appeared to all men
- ii) it teaches to say, "no" to ungodliness
- iii) it teaches to say, "no" to worldly passions
- iv) it teaches to live a self-controlled life
- v) it teaches to live an upright life
- vi) it teaches to live a godly life

All in this present age. Now if the grace of God cannot restrain you from willful, premeditated sin and all manner of ungodliness, then it will not cleanse you from those sins either. Why? Because in deliberately sinning after you have known the truth, the writer of Hebrews tell us you do the following:

i) you trample the Son of God underfoot
ii) you treat as an unholy thing the blood of the covenant that sanctified you
iii) you insult the Spirit of grace

and as such you can expect nothing but God's judgment.

Will you continue to be blinded by your sin?

Will you not immediately forsake your sin so as to behold the Father in His justice?

❖ **Sin saps away strength:**

"O Lord, have mercy on me in my anguish. My eyes are red from weeping; my health is broken from sorrow. I am pining away with grief; my years are shortened, drained away because of sadness. *My sins have sapped my strength; I stoop with sorrow and with shame*" **(Psalm 31:10, TLB, emphasis added).**

"For day and night your hand was heavy upon me; my strength was sapped as in the heat of summer (Psalm 32: 4).

There is nothing that saps away both physical and spiritual strength like sin. In whatever form it is practiced, sin will drain away the strength and power to perform. Don't you see why sinners turn to drugs and to the satanic supernatural for power to perform?

❖ **Sin robs a man of his capacity to hear God:**

"Hear this, you foolish and senseless people, who have eyes but do not see, who have ears but do not hear" (Jeremiah 5:21).

Sin blocks a man's spiritual hearing and capacity to see and discern spiritual things. It deprives you of the capacity to discern the moves of God in your environment.

- ❖ **Sin disqualifies a man from his rights as a child of God: "Reuben, you are my oldest son, the child of my vigorous youth. You are the head of the list in rank and in honor. 4 But you are unruly as the wild waves of the sea, and you shall be first no longer. I am demoting you, for you slept with one of my wives and thus dishonored me" (Genesis 49:3-4,TLB).**

Cain forfeited his rights as the first born of Adam because of his sin. That is why the ancestry of man is traced through Seth. Reuben forfeited his rights as the first born of Jacob because of his sin. Sin demotes a man in rank before the Almighty God. Every sin you commit deliberately only takes you lower and lower spiritually.

As children of God, we are meant to soar like eagles, rising with each passing day to spiritual heights. Sin only demotes you and prevents you from soaring. Sin affects your destiny negatively; it darkens your path and makes your future uncertain. Sin is no friend to the child of God, no matter what it appears to offer.

Deliberate, premeditated sin is the greatest horror that can happen to anyone. It is the greatest dishonor you can give God and the greatest disfavor you can do yourself. The pleasure of sin is the greatest folly you can accept. Reuben slept with his father's wife just once but that was sufficient to mar his whole destiny. Sin does not need a second chance to ruin a man permanently. Reuben remained Jacobs's son but he forfeited his place as first-born.

- ❖ **Sin robs a man of his capacity to pull others along God's path:**

"Then I will teach transgressors your ways, and sinners will turn back to you" (Psalm 51:13).

After David had sinned, he pleaded with God for forgiveness and also that he would be able, once more, to teach others the ways of God for them to turn from their sins to God. If you live in sin, no matter the form, no matter how much you preach, the best you can do is to turn sinners to a religious system, making then even worse than they were.

You can never lead someone to Christ while living in sin. That will be the greatest deception of all time. There are many people today living in this kind of deception; they live in sin and then still go about preaching the Gospel. Their goal is to get people make a commitment to a system other than to Christ. Did the Lord not confront the Pharisees and the teachers of the law of traveling long distances to make a single convert who became twice fit for hell than before?

- ❖ **Sin robs a man of his authority:**

When God created man, he gave man authority and dominion over the rest of terrestrial creation (see Genesis 1) but as soon as man sinned and rebelled against God, he lost that authority and dominion (see Genesis 3) and today man is threatened and frightened by the smallest of animals.

About Ephraim, the Lord says, **"When Ephraim spoke, men trembled; he was exalted in Israel. But he became guilty of Baal worship and died (Hosea 13:1).** Dying here talks of losing his authority. Until he became guilty, he had his authority as the firstborn, but once he became guilty he died in terms of his authority.

- ❖ **Sin disqualifies a man from prayer:**

> "When you spread out your hands in prayer, I will hide my eyes from you; even if you offer many prayers, I will not listen. Your hands are full of blood; wash and make yourselves clean. Take your evil deeds out of my sight! Stop doing wrong" (Isaiah 1:15-16)

> "If I regard iniquity in my heart, the Lord will not hear me" (Psalm 66:18, KJV).

Sin in a man's heart or life disqualifies him from prayer, because no matter how much, with what intensity, and for how long he prayers, God will not and does not listen. If God will not, and does not hear a man's prayer what need is there to pray, if answers to your prayers will not be received?

- ❖ **Sin seeks nothing but to master the sinner and enslave him:**
  "If you do what is right, will you not be accepted? But if you do not do what is right, sin is crouching at your door; it desires to have you, but you must master it" (Genesis 4:7).
  'Jesus replied, "I tell you the truth, everyone who sins is a slave to sin"' (John 8:34).

When God forewarned Cain not to give in to the pressure from the sin of jealousy, He understood that giving in to that would only lead to a chain of sins. Cain's chain sin started by failure to do the right thing. We can illustrate the chain as follows: feeling of rejection to anger to jealousy to hatred to murder to lying. What about David's sin with Bathsheba? From idleness to lust to adultery to getting someone drunk to murder to seizing someone's wife.

Sin is a chain chemical reaction. Once started, it becomes difficult to stop until the reaction is complete. No addict ever started out as an addict. It started as fun and gradually sin got hold of him and overcame him until he was mastered by the addiction. Sin seeks nothing but to enslave the sinner. There is no greater bondage than that to sin.

- ❖ **Sin is the greatest weight a man can carry:**

"Son of man, say to the house of Israel, `This is what you are saying: "Our offenses and sins weigh us down, and we are wasting away because of them. How then can we live?" (Ezekiel 33:10)

There's nothing that weighs and wears a man out like sin does. Its weight is crushing. The one who refuses to repent from his sins will waste away (Psalm 32:3). Is that not why the Savior called, "come to me, all you who are weary and burdened, and I will give you rest" (Matthew 11:28)? For how long shall you be crushed by the weight of your sins? Is it not time you confess and forsake them so that you can find rest for your soul?

- ❖ **Sin deprives a man of his harvest:**

"if my steps have turned from the path, if my heart has been led by my eyes, or if my hands have been defiled, then may others eat what I have sown, and may my crops be uprooted….It is a fire that burns to Destruction; it would have uprooted my harvest" (Job 31:7-8, 12).

"But see, we are slaves today, slaves in the land you gave our forefathers so they could eat its fruit and the other good things it produces. [37] Because of our sins, its abundant harvest goes to the kings you have placed over us. They rule over our bodies and our cattle as they please. We are in great distress" (Nehemiah 9:36-37).

There's a lot of teaching going on today about seed sowing. I have heard many preachers encourage people to keep sowing, as they would one day reap their harvest. The sad thing about this is that I have never heard anybody taught on the fact that a man can be deprived of his harvest, no matter how much he sows, if he is living in sin. Sin destroys a man's harvest.

It is futile to encourage people to keep sowing without pointing out to them the pest that destroys their harvest. Do you remember in the time of the Judges how the Israelites were impoverished by the Midianites and the Amalekites who constantly destroyed their crops because of Israel's sin? (See judges 6). Sin in your life is like those Midianites and Amalekites destroying the harvest of whatever you sow.

Maybe you are reaping something, but I tell you, it is nothing compared to what you could reap were the harvest not destroyed. Do you want to reap your full harvest? Depart from all known sin, if not you shall continue to sow in vain. Do not listen to those who encourage you to keep sowing without warning you that sin in your life destroys your harvest.

A case study
I'd like us to study the life of one particular man in scripture, so as to drive home what we have been saying here and build a premise for our next chapter.

For a moment, I want you to read through Genesis chapter thirty-eight. Do not continue until you have read through the chapter.
Chapter thirty-seven narrates the story of Joseph and his brothers, how he was sold by his brothers into slavery in Egypt at the suggestion of Judah, instead of the intended abandonment and eventual death in the waterless cistern.

To speculate, the brothers got into a covenant that no one was to let their father know of what had happened to Joseph. Judah, seeing their father in distress because of the "death" of their brother could not help but leave the house to seek for refuge from his guilt. He went down to Hirah of Adullam.

Adullam means "refuge". In going there Judah thought he was going to find refuge from his sin against his brother and thus, against his father. He thought leaving home was going to provide the solution to his guilt. I want you to realize that Judah's attempt to seek for refuge away from home only landed him further into trouble.

There is no refuge for you away from home- the presence of your loving Father in heaven. There is no other cover for sin but the Blood of the Lamb that was slain; there is no hiding place for your sin but Jesus Himself. There are many, like Judah who have left home because of the guilt of sin. Home is the very place God meant to be shelter from the pressures from without.

Why do we say Judah only got into more trouble? Because his whole stay at Adullam was a miserable one. Judah met a Canaanite girl to whom he got married. She was the daughter of Shua. Now, Shua means prosperity. In marrying Shua's daughter he was making a covenant with prosperity. Did his marriage with "the offspring of prosperity" bring him any prosperity? No! It only led to one calamity after another; the death of his wife and two sons.

My brother, my sister, that which appears as though it is going to give you happiness and prosperity away from the Savior will only land you into misery. There is no lasting or true prosperity apart from the Savior. True and lasting prosperity is that of the whole man, and that can only be found in Christ. Judah had every opportunity to confess his sins to his father but didn't, may be because of the covenant with his brothers.

Do you find yourself in the same situation, you committed a sin or got yourself into some situation, which you feel guilty about, but you are afraid to expose it because of some covenant you made? Your heavenly Father knows about it, He has power to nullify that covenant by the blood of the Eternal Covenant in Jesus.

Go to some spiritual authority and expose it to him. That will help you break free from the torments of your sin. Do not sit quietly and groan under the weight and agony of guilt. You can be set free. When Judah refused to expose his sin, thinking he was going to find refuge somewhere else, it let him at some later time into incest with his own daughter in- law. Now, the Bible says, **"Flee from sexual immorality. All other sins a man commits are outside his body, but he who sins sexually sins against his own body. [19] Do you not know that your body is a temple of the Holy Spirit, who is in you, whom you have received from God? You are not your own; [20] you were bought at a price. Therefore honor God with your body" (1Corinthians 6:18-20).**

That which a man gives out through sexual immorality cannot be recovered. The greatest folly is the pleasure of sexual sin. The Bible says, "you were bought at a price" meaning you are not your own, your body belongs to another, whom you must honor. That another is God. Your body is the temple of the Holy Spirit, so before you do anything with it ask yourself, "Will this make the Holy Spirit comfortable in His temple?" Nothing, which damages the temple or grieves Him who dwells there is good for you.

Allow your view of your body to change from "my body" to "His temple" and eventually the way you treat it is going to change for good. The price of your body is worth the blood of Jesus. Will you dare exchange it for anything less? God forbid!

There's a part of you, which goes out through sexual immorality, which cannot be recuperated. Sexual sin does untold harm and damage to the temple of the Holy Spirit. In committing fornication with Tamar, Judah gave away the following:

1) His seal
2) His seal's cord
3) His staff.

Each of the above things represents what a man loses as a result of sexual sin. Let us examine them in details.

The seal

The seal symbolizes the following:

i) Mark of authenticity: in ancient times, a man's seal represented his identity. It was also used to identify a man's property and ratify transactions. In giving away his seal, Judah gave away his identity. Does the Bible not say, "He who unites himself with a prostitute is one with her in body" (1 Corinthians 6:16)? Sexual immorality brings about the putting on of another's identity. That is why anyone who begins to commit sexual immorality begins to behave in a strange way. Parents of young men and women who have been involved in this sin know what I am saying.

ii) Used to prevent unauthorized access to documents and property: by giving away his seal, Judah had no means of protecting his documents and property from trespassers. Thus, we see that sexual sin makes someone open to demonic attacks and attack by disease. It makes even a man's property and possessions open to the attacks of satan and his host of demons.

iii) Proof of delegated authority: in those days, any man of standing had a seal, which was proof of his authority. In delegating someone, it sufficed to give him your seal and that was enough to prove that you have delegated your authority to him. Now in Luke 10:19, the Lord says, **"I have given you authority to trample on snakes and scorpions, and to overcome all the power of the enemy; nothing will harm you."** Like Judah, when you sin sexually you forfeit that authority to the devil.

The cord

The cord was used to hang a seal to a man's neck or round his waist. The cord is used as a symbol of life (see Ecclesiastes 12:6). When you have a cord attached to anything you can lead and manipulate that thing even from a distance to whatever direction you want. Sexual immorality provides a cord through which the devil manipulates and controls a life. That is why sexual sin is hardly ever dealt with until this cord is severed in the spiritual. Have you ever seen a grown man or woman powerless before the sexual sin partner who is of no match? That is the reason why.

The staff

The staff also is symbolic of the following:

i) Authority
ii) Power to discipline and correct

iii) Support and direction

In giving away his staff, he gave away his power to discipline and correct, and also his sense of direction. Is that not why in an office where a boss is having an affair with his secretary you find all manner of chaos? In a school where the principal has affairs with students you find the reign of indiscipline?

No matter how much Judah tried afterwards to regain these things he gave out, it was to no avail (v22). **"Then Judah said, 'let her keep what she has, or we will become a laughing-stock…"** (v23).

Sexual sin is the greatest catalyst to pride and arrogance. Judah was afraid of becoming a laughing-stock. Is there any greater shame and disgrace than for a man to have lost his God-given identity, authority and direction in life? Judah labored so hard to appear before man what he wasn't. He wanted to appear as a man of integrity and rectitude meanwhile he was the total opposite. I want to let you know that, what matters is what a man appears before God and His angels and not what he or she may appear before man.

Heaven rates a fornicator and adulterer as a loaf of bread (Proverbs 6:26). If becoming a laughing-stock will help you regain your identity, authority and direction in life why not become one? It is better to become a laughing- stock before man and be a hero before God than to appear a hero before man and be a waif before God.

Chapter 13

How to deal with sin

Having seen what sin does to a man irrespective of sex, age, status, race or culture, let us see how we can slay this monster in our individual lives. The Bible says,

"Therefore, since we are surrounded by such a great cloud of witnesses, let us throw off everything that hinders and the sin that so easily entangles, and let us run with perseverance the race marked out for us" (Hebrews 12:1).

"Put to death, therefore, whatever belongs to your earthly nature: sexual immorality, impurity, lust, evil desires and greed, which is idolatry" (Colossians 3:5).

To deal with sin, the foundation lies in realizing that no sin can ever be hidden from God. God sees all your sins.

"But if you fail to do this, you will be sinning against the Lord; and you may be sure that your sin will find you out" (Numbers 32:23).

> "Lord, you see what they are doing. You have noted each evil act" (Psalm 10:14a, TLB).

No one ever succeeded to hide his sin:

Adam did not succeed to hide his sin from God.

Cain did not succeed to hide his sin from God, even when he thought he was all alone with Abel in the field.

Judah did not succeed to hide his sin with Tamar. He hid it for three months but the truth eventually came out.

Joseph's brothers hid their sin for about twenty years but the truth eventually came out.

David hid his sin with Bathsheba for over a year but the truth eventually came out.

Let me tell you,

You will not succeed either, to cover your sin before the eyes of the all-watching and all-seeing God. It is either you expose and renounce your sins or your sin will expose you.

Having seen that sin can never be hidden from God, we can now proceed to see how we can deal with sin.

Sin must be confessed specifically

Sin can never be treated as a general thing. Whatever form it takes, sin must be confessed specifically. The Bible says,

> **"If we confess our sins, he is faithful and just and will forgive us our sins and purify us from all unrighteousness" (1 John 1:9).**

.

> **"When I kept silent, my bones wasted away through my groaning all day long. For day and night your hand was heavy**

upon me; my strength was sapped as in the heat of summer. Then I acknowledged my sin to you and did not cover up my iniquity. I said, "I will confess my transgressions to the LORD"--and you forgave the guilt of my sin" (Psalm 32:3-5)

Thus, without the proper confession, there is no forgiveness. God's forgiveness through the atoning work of the "Lamb that was slain" is available to all mankind, yet there are countless people moving about the streets who have not obtained this forgiveness. Why? Because it is available only to those, who will accept it, through confession and forsaking of sins.

"If anyone is guilty in any of these ways, <u>he must confess in what way he has sinned</u>." (Leviticus 5:5. emphasis, mine).

God never made any room for some general confession of sin. If you are asking for forgiveness you must state what you should be forgiven for. Don't you remember the blind man in the Gospels? "He called out, 'Jesus, son of David, have mercy on me!'" (Luke 18:38) "When he came near, Jesus asked him, 'what do you want me to do for you?'" (Luke 18:40b). Confession, like any other manner of praying has to be specific. Maybe you are wondering about the sin you have forgotten and the ones you did commit ignorantly? Well I just want you to know that ignorance is not a passport to sin:

"If a person sins and does what is forbidden in any of the LORD's commands, even though he does not know it, he is guilty and will be held responsible" (Leviticus 5:17).

Until sin is confessed and forsaken, the sinner remains guilty. That is why we are supposed to spend time with God daily in prayer and the study of His word. As we spend time with Him, He will bring to mind the sins we have committed unknown to us, or those we may have forgotten so that they should be repented of, renounced and abandoned.

It is the responsibility of the Spirit to show us the sins that are still standing against us, but it is absolutely ours to bring ourselves into the right condition for Him to show us. So, spend time with God daily in openhearted fellowship.

How is confession done?

The following steps are necessary for confession to be thorough and complete:

1) **Acknowledge your sin**.

When a man refuses to acknowledge his or her sin, he or she provokes the judgment of God. **"You say, 'I am innocent; he is not angry with me.' But I will pass judgment on you because you say, 'I have not sinned'" (Jeremiah 2:35)**. Acknowledging your sin is the first step to receiving forgiveness. Without it, there can be no true confession and therefore no forgiveness.

> **"Only acknowledge your guilt-- you have rebelled against the LORD your God, you have scattered your favors to foreign gods under every spreading tree, and have not obeyed me,' declares the LORD" (Jeremiah 3:13).**

> **"Then I acknowledged my sin to you and did not cover up my iniquity. I said, "I will confess my transgressions to the LORD"-- and you forgave the guilt of my sin" (Psalm 32:5).**

To acknowledge your sin will mean you claiming full responsibility for your sin without trying to shift the blame to someone else or to the circumstances. Do not be like Adam. Acknowledging your sin means believing in your heart that if God were to judge you that will be Justice.

2) **Ask for forgiveness:**

"Forgive us our sins…" (Luke 11:4a).

You must ask for forgiveness for you to obtain it. Acknowledging your sin and not asking for forgiveness amounts to nothing. He said, "Ask and you shall be given." What then is the basis on which to ask for forgiveness?

The basis for forgiveness

> **"In him we have redemption through his blood, the forgiveness of sins, in accordance with the riches of God's grace" (Ephesians 1:7)**

The number one basis for forgiveness is the atoning work accomplished on Calvary by God's own Son. Without it, you and I have no mandate to ask for forgiveness. It is in accordance with the riches of God's grace that we can ever be forgiven. Out of Christ there is no forgiveness no matter the rituals or penance that is carried out.

The number two basis for forgiveness is that you also forgive: **"Forgive us our debts, as we also have forgiven our debtors." (Matthew 6:12).** Until you have forgiven everyone who has sinned against you in any way, you cannot be forgiven by God. When you refuse to forgive those who wrong you, God counts all your previous sins against you as depicted in the parable of the unforgiving servant (see Matthew 18:21-35). The servant had already been forgiven, but when he refused to forgive his fellow servant, his master annulled the forgiveness that had been granted him, and the Lord said, **"this is how my heavenly Father** will treat each of you unless you forgive your brother from your heart" (Matthew 18:35).

Refuse at any cost, the "luxury' of holding grudges against whosoever.

3) **Ask for cleansing:**

"Wash away my iniquity and cleanse me from all my sin" (Psalm 51:2).

After obtaining forgiveness you must asked God to cleanse you from the guilt and effect of sin.

4) **Ask for God to blot out your sin:**

"For I know my transgressions, and my sin is always before me." (Psalm 51:3).

Unless your sin is blotted out it will remain in the records and will therefore stand before you. You must ask for the sin to be blotted out so that you do not see it again. **"According to your great compassion blot out my transgressions" (Psalm 51:1b).** If it is not blotted out, though God may have forgiven you, you will have the tendency to always think of it and this will render you ineffective.

5) **Forsake your sin:**

"He that covereth his sins shall not prosper; but whoso confesseth and *forsaketh* them shall have mercy" (Proverbs 28:13, KJV, emphasis mine).

For you to fine total forgiveness, you must forsake your sins i.e. you must renounce and abandon them. Confession without forsaking of sin has no effect; it is incomplete.

Sin must be amended for

In handling sin, there is a part which is hardly ever mentioned. Though sin is primarily against God, it is manifested in ways that fellow man is affected. Thus, for sin to be properly dealt with, amends must be made. Proverbs 14:9a says, **"Fools mock at making amends for sin" (NIV).** Anyone who refuses to make amends for sin, where possible, is considered, by God to be a fool. Seek to make amends for sin wherever it is possible.

> **"When he thus sins and becomes guilty, he must return what he has stolen or taken by extortion, or what was entrusted to him, or the lost property he found, [5] or whatever it was he swore falsely about. He must make restitution in full, add a fifth of the value to it and give it all to the owner on the day he presents his guilt offering" (Leviticus 6:4-5).**

> **"The LORD said to Moses, [6] "Say to the Israelites: `When a man or woman wrongs another in any way and so is unfaithful to the LORD, that person is guilty [7] and must confess the sin he has committed.** *He must make full restitution for his wrong*, **add one fifth to it and give it all to the person he has wronged" (Numbers 5:5-7).**

> **"And if I say to the wicked man, `You will surely die,' but he then turns away from his sin and does what is just and right--** [15] *if he gives back what he took in pledge for a loan, returns what he has stolen*, **follows the decrees that give life, and does no evil, he will surely live; he will not die.** [16] **None of the sins he has committed will**

be remembered against him. He has done what is just and right; he will surely live" (Ezekiel 33:14-16).

From simple wrongs, to theft, to murder, sin must be amended for. In some cases this will entail just exposing your sin to a spiritual authority so he can pray with you and for you.

When all the above steps are followed, you can claim His promise, which says, **"for I will forgive their wickedness, and will remember their sins no more" (Hebrew 8:12).**

> **"Who is a God like you, who pardons sin and forgives the transgression of the remnant of his inheritance? You do not stay angry forever but delight to show mercy. You will again have compassion on us; you will tread our sins underfoot and hurl all our iniquities into the depths of the sea"(Micah 7:18-19).**

That is the God you are serving. Won't you lift up those hands and praise him?

Maybe you have not yet known Him as your Saviour and Lord. It is only in Him you can find forgiveness, not in some religious system. You can't be reconciled to the Father by any other means but by falling at the feet of Jesus, inviting Him into your life as Lord and Saviour. When this happens, He gives you the power (right) to become a child of God (see John 1:12-13, Romans 10:9-11). At this very moment, you can invite Him into your life, do it now! Repeat this prayer, "Lord Jesus, I repent of all my sins and ask you to forgive me, cleans me and make me your child. Come into my heart and empower me to live for you. In your holt name I ask, amen"

Chapter 14

Knowing who and what you are

In the previous chapters, we have put forth the nature of the conflict, the enemy we are fighting against, his weapons and strategies; we have also put forth our mandate, our weapons and the potentials of our weapons. In this chapter, we are going to look at the soldier who is using the weapon i.e. we are looking at you as the wielder of the weapon before we look at how to wield your weapon as a soldier.

As you prepare to use your weapons I want you to understand that with God you are indomitable. Omnipotence is on your side and therefore, no other power can overcome you. God said to Israel,

> **"So do not fear, for I am with you; do not be dismayed, for I am your God. I will strengthen you and help you; I will uphold**

you with my righteous right hand. All who rage against you will surely be ashamed and disgraced; those who oppose you will be as nothing and perish. Though you search for your enemies, you will not find them. Those who wage war against you will be as nothing at all. For I am the LORD, your God, who takes hold of your right hand and says to you, do not fear; I will help you" (Isaiah 41:10-13).

In the above scripture passage, there are a number of commands, assurances, and promises: let's bring them out so you can see for yourself what God has declared about you;

The commands are
- do not fear
- do not be dismayed

The assurances are
- I am with you
- I am your God
- I am the LORD

The promises are
- I will strengthen you
- I will help you
- I will uphold you with my righteous right hand
- Your enemies will be disgraced
- Your enemies will perish
- Your enemies will be brought to naught

Now, if you are to remain an overcomer, you must keep fear and discouragement far from you. Fear and discouragement are two dangerous enemies in your camp, you must not permit them to operate in your life.

Fear paralyzes and incapacitates a man.

Fear breaks your defence mechanism and makes you vulnerable to defeat and failure.

When you give in to fear you forfeit God's promises.

Fear grounds your potentials.

Fear is dangerously contagious.

Fear is a spirit which is not from God.

Omnipotence cannot manifest on your behalf when you give in to fear.

God is helpless to help the fearful.

Fear and love cannot co-exist.

Fear deprives you of soundness of mind.

As you face every challenge in life, you must believe that omnipotence is with you, you must believe that omniscience is with you, and you must believe that omnipresence is with you.

In this battle of life, God has promised to strengthen you. To strengthen means to energize, it means to fortify, it means to render capable and able to do or to withstand. It means to enable. Live daily knowing that you have divine enabling at your disposal. Live daily knowing that you have a fortification from heaven which nothing can overcome. The Holy Ghost energizing power is for you.

Heaven will render you capable to overcome every difficulty you face in this life. Every pressure in life from the enemy onslaught, heaven will enable you to withstand. They might be financial pressures or difficulties, emotional pressures or difficulties, mental pressures or difficulties, moral pressures or difficulties, spiritual pressures or difficulties, and emotional pressures and difficulties. All these areas are equally important because once the enemy succeeds in one area of your life, there is the possibility that he will overcome you in the other areas too.

All who have made it in this race have always have God as their strength. If you too must succeed and triumph, you must daily appropriate the Lord as your strength. The psalmist knew God as his strength (Psalm 18:1, 28:7, 59:17, 73:26, 118:14). Moses knew God as his strength (Exodus 15:2). Isaiah knew God as his strength (Isaiah 12:2). Habakkuk called God his strength (Habakkuk 3:19). Paul knew God as the One who strengthened him (Philippians 4:13). You too, have to appropriate and declare the Lord as your strength!

God has also promised to help you. Help here means to be a part of a particular burden, task, or responsibility. God wants to be an integral part of what you do. He wants to be "hands on" with you in the battles of life. Again, the psalmist knew the Lord as his help,, his ever present help (Psalm 33:20, Psalm 46:1), Samuel knew God as his help (1Samuel 7:12), Paul knew God as his help (Acts 26:22). Live daily knowing that God is your help and life will be far more exciting than you have ever imagined.

He will uphold you

To uphold means to sustain, to support, and to maintain. God wants to sustain, support and maintain you financially, emotionally, mentally, socially, physically, and spiritually. He wants His sustenance to permeate every area of your being. It means He will maintain your power (Psalm

37:17), keep you from falling (Psalm 37:24), protect you (Psalm 140:12), and supply you with all that you need (Psalm 146:7). Your only responsibility is to believe what God says, then leave the rest to Him. He is too true to lie and too faithful to fail.

God says your enemies will be disgraced! It is His promise, no matter their number, no matter their weaponry, no matter their strategies, what heaven has decreed for them is disgrace. As you believe and act on this you will begin to see the open disgrace of your enemies. I feel like shouting! Now let's look at what the sovereign Lord says about you somewhere else:

> **"Do not be afraid of them, for I am with you and will rescue you," declares the LORD... Today I have made you a fortified city, an iron pillar and a bronze wall to stand against the whole land--against the kings of Judah, its officials, its priests and the people of the land. ^{19} They will fight against you but will not overcome you, for I am with you and will rescue you," declares the LORD." (Jeremiah 1:8,18-19)**

Here, we find the Lord making some very far reaching declarations about you. A declaration is a statement of purpose and commitment.

The Lord God says, "do not be afraid of them" and "they will fight". To whom is them and they in the above verse referring to? I believe to all your enemies; satan and his host of demons, satanic human agents, sickness, poverty, failure, defeat etc.

The fact that God says to rescue you shows that there is danger. To rescue means to snatch away, to deliver, to save, to preserve, and to defend. God will snatch you away from their traps, He will defend you from their attacks, and He will preserve all that pertains to you. The assurance of God's presence should be a comforting reality.

You should be able to face every situation knowing that God is with you therefore, the enemy can accomplish nothing in you, on you or through you.

Jeremiah had been called to face an entire backslidden nation and confront them with the truth of God's word. It was one man against an entire nation, yet God told him they would fight against him and not be able to overcome him. Is that not invincibility? Is that not being unbeatable? I want you to know that though all of hell be let loose, because God is with you, their schemes will amount to nothing.

You are invincible

God says He has made you a fortified city, He has made you an iron pillar, and He has made you a bronze wall. A fortified city is permanently set against every enemy infiltration and invasion. You can live in a fortified city with all the sense of security and confidence. An iron pillar cannot easily be bended nor moved. A bronze wall cannot be broken down or scaled over by the enemy. Heaven has rendered you impregnable; unbeatable, invincible, indomitable and "unovercomable".

You cannot be overcome by satan. You cannot be overcome by witches. You cannot be overcome by sickness and disease. That is what heaven has decreed for you. And because heaven rules over the whole universe you have the mandate to impose that decree in your domain. Heaven has not said that they will never fight against you. On the contrary it has promised that they will fight but victory shall be yours.

Satan may marshal all his army and lay siege against your life, but they shall not overcome you because, even as heaven has decreed victory for you, so it has decreed failure and defeat for the devil. I want to let you know that the Counsel of heaven sat and passed a judgement on satan that has never been reversed; the devil has been declared an eternal failure and a permanent loser.

The Bible says, a student cannot be greater than his master, so if satan has been decreed a permanent loser all his followers have been decreed losers and failures. If you read Genesis 3:14-15, the Lord told him (the devil) that he was cursed above all living things. God decreed for him to crawl- that is the position or posture of someone who has been defeated. But, about the saints God says, "they shall mount up with wings as eagles… they shall run…they shall walk" (Isaiah 40:31). So, you are meant to fly, or run, or walk. Your enemy is doomed to crawl.

The Lord said something more humiliating about the devil, that he will eat dust all the days of his life. His delicacies should be what you have already trampled on and walked over, but for you God says, He prepares a table before you in the presence of you enemies. The sad thing is that for some of God's children the devil seems to have turned the tables, he feeds on the delicacies while they feed on the dust.

Hey! From today you know what heaven has declared for satan as food. Each time he wants to feed on your finances tell him "hey boy you are mistaken, you cannot feed on my finances, heaven says the dust must be your food" then command him to go eat the dust. Whatever is of yours he wants to feed on tell him he has no right to do that, heaven has decreed nothing for him as food but the dust.

I want you to begin to confess that you are more than conquerors; declare that you are invincible, declare that you are unbeatable; declare that you cannot be overcome by one who has been declared a failure.

The right attitude

Now, listen once again to what heaven says to you, "**Be strong and courageous. Do not be afraid or terrified because of them, for the LORD your God goes with you; he will never leave you nor forsake you**" **(Deuteronomy 31:6).**

Heaven wants you to maintain an attitude of strength and courage so that you will be effective in all you do. Fear and discouragement are husband and wife who will always give birth to defeat, failure, confusion, and frustration. They themselves are offspring of doubt and unbelief.

To overcome fear and discouragement you must keep your focus on what the word of God declares about you and on His presence and companionship! Strength and courage are the keys to the release of omnipotence. If omnipotence must act on your behalf you must be strong and courageous. That is why He says "let the weak say I am strong" (Joel 3:10b) and "strengthen those feeble hands" (Isaiah 35:3a).

Face every new day with the strength, courage and knowledge that omnipotence will never leave you, that omnipresence will never abandon you. The word never has a threefold implication. It means in no time, in no circumstance, and in no place. You remember the Lord Jesus said, "… I am with you always..." Always, here means everywhere, every time, and in everything! That is the commitment of omnipotence, omnipresence, and omniscience to you!

Satan will do everything to robe you of your strength and courage by trying to get you panic-stricken. Once he succeeds to do that omnipotence becomes helpless as far as you are concerned. Strength and courage activate omnipotence on your behalf and sets it into motion against your enemies. The presence of God-His manifest presence i.e. activated omnipresence is your trump card against the enemy. God is everywhere and His power is everywhere, what you need is His activated presence and power. It is what makes the difference!

You are an imperialist

Now, take a look at what the Lord said to Joshua, **"I will give you every place where you set your foot, as I promised Moses. 4 Your territory will extend from the desert to Lebanon, and from the great river, the Euphrates--all the Hittite country--to the Great Sea on the west. 5 No one will be able to stand up against you all the days of your life. As I was with Moses, so I will be with you; I will never leave you nor forsake you" (Joshua 1: 3-5).**

God has declared you an imperialist; you have the right to possess every place that your foot touches. I want you to begin to set your feet into your inheritance of financial, social, material, emotional and above all spiritual abundance. Picture yourself setting your foot on the contested territory of your inheritance and begin to claim the whole land allotted to you by the Counsel of heaven- the fullness of your inheritance in Christ Jesus.

"No one" means all without exception no mater how big, no matter how trained, no matter how sophisticated his weapons or machinery may be; within the territory of your inheritance no one has the right to contest with you.

"Will be able to stand up against you"
Let me tell you what that means:
- no one will have the ability to stand up against you
- no one will have what is required to stand up against you
- no one who attempts will succeed to stand up against you
- anyone who attempts to stand up against you will end up taking a crawling position.

For no one reason should the devil, or any of his servants, be able to stand up against you. The posture heaven has decreed for them is the crawling posture. That means they must bow down before you. Everything in the domain of your rule and inheritance must bow and submit to you.

The Bible does not say no one will attempt to stand up against you, but that even though they may attempt to, they will not be able as long as you have God's life in you. That is why spiritual vitality is paramount in spiritual warfare and victorious living. Feed on the word of God through Bible reading, study, and meditation on the Word.

"As I was… so I will be…"
God longs daily to show His unchanging nature to mankind and to principalities and powers. He longs passionately to reveal to man that, as He was yesterday so He is today, and will be tomorrow. He is the God who spans eternity. He longs to demonstrate the unchanging nature of His power, His justice, and His infinite love. In Joshua 3:7 He says "…I am…as I was"

He is the same yesterday, today and forever! If you will just make yourself available, then you will become God's weapon or instrument through which He will demonstrate His power, justice and faithfulness.

If you allow all these to sink deep down into you; that the God who has never failed will not fail you, that the God who has never lost a battle will not lose any on your behalf; you will forever be victorious.

Chapter 15

Wielding your weapons

No matter how sophisticated and destructive a weapon may be, if the one using it hasn't any mastery of the weapon, there is no way the weapon can function to the fullest of its potentials and capabilities. One could even say that the greater the potentials of a weapon the more self-devastating it could be in the hands of one who has not learned how to use it.

The first thing I want to say is that the weapons we have can only be effective as we use them through God for Kingdom purposes. Never use any of the aforementioned weapons for selfish reasons. Do not use them because someone has offended you. The target of your weapons is not human beings but the devil.

Do not become jealous of someone else's property and then use these weapons through soulish prayers. If you do that, you will not be using the weapons through God, but will be sending them into the air for the devil to use against people. Be sure that each time you are using these mighty spiritual weapons their effects will lead to the advancement of the Kingdom of God and not some personal kingdom.

Now, remember each of the weapons we mentioned above has a counterpart in the physical. To effectively use such weapons, you must know how the physical counterpart works. For example, fire is used in the physical to burn things. If the spiritual situation needs that something be burned, then can you demand that fire consume the situation you face! Here, we need a lot of wisdom as the Holy Spirit leads. For example, if you realise you are up against a spiritual wall blocking your forward movement in whatever domain of your life you can command the earthquake of the Lord to shake down the wall.

If you are to destroy enemy spy satellites you can command the east wind of the Lord to blow them off their trajectory and shatter them to pieces. The same can be applied to spy cameras; telescopes etc. after blowing them off, if you want them to be permanently destroyed you can then release fire to consume such apparels.

You can also command lightning to strike all stray space or air vessels which are intruding your spiritual domain. Also, just as you can scatter physical enemies by throwing physical grenades into their midst, so you can release spiritual grenades into enemy camps. Such prayers are best between 12 midnight and 3 am when they are usually gathered. If you know the specific place of their gathering you can direct these weapons at them.

You can intercept the transportation of their illegal goods by releasing the east wind of the Lord to damage all such vessels which may be transporting human souls or blood to supply their blood banks.

You can rain down fire upon satanic altars raised against the people and the work of God. You can also release spiritual teargas into their midst. You can pull down their watchtowers so that they will not be able to monitor you from there using their satanic telescopes.

You know, the devil assigns spy demons who monitor your movement and give back reports. To make this point very clear turn with me to the Book. David prayed,

> **"Keep me as the apple of your eye; hide me in the shadow of your wings from the wicked who assail me, from my mortal enemies who surround me. They close up their callous hearts, and their mouths speak with arrogance. They have tracked me down, they now surround me, with eyes alert, to throw me to the ground" (Psalm 17:9-11).**

You see, David was very aware of his enemies. He knew there were foes that sought his life and wanted his ruin. I want you to know that there are spirit beings assailing you. There are spirit beings tracking you with the intention to throw you down.

When the Lord taught me this, then I realise the need to always pray and incapacitate their spy machinery by striking such monitoring spirits with blindness. You can also render them deaf mute so that they can neither hear nor speak and so their mission will be permanently frustrated. I have often pronounced a decree that no two of such monitoring spirits will be able to agree on any report to give concerning me.

They can insert microphones into your spiritual environment so as to monitor your every conversation and prayer. You will have to pray and blow off such devices used in spiritual spying by the enemy. You can carve out a spiritual zone and declare it a no-go-zone for satan and his demons and human agents. When you do this, you can give heaven the mandate to place coast guards to arrest and permanently bind intruders and trespassers.

You remember how the Lord released hailstones against the enemy army. When you sense you are under siege you too can ask heaven to release hailstones against the enemies who are gathered around your walls or gates.

There is something the Lord Jesus taught about the influence of the heavenly bodies in human affairs. Listen to what He said:

> **"There will be signs in the sun, moon and stars. On the earth, nations will be in anguish and perplexity at the roaring and tossing of the sea. [26] Men will faint from terror, apprehensive of what is coming on the world, for the heavenly bodies will be shaken"(Luke 21:25-26)**

The signs in the sun, moon and stars are what will be causing the anguish on the earth. And that is what the devil is doing today. He is using the heavenly bodies to greatly influence human activities here on earth. That is why there are some sickness and diseases that come upon you when the sun is rising, others when it is setting, other things just happen with respect to the size of the moon. They are like an endless cycle of events.

For others the roaring of the sea during high tides bring them untold trouble and physical distress. That is why you must pray at regular intervals, if not daily, dismantling the programs of the enemy put in the heavenly bodies or the sea to work against you. You can command the programmes to crash and abort.

Conclusion

You may need to do a second, third, and even a fourth reading to properly grasp and appropriate everything we have shared in this book. You may suffer some scars in this battlefield of life, but one thing is sure, the Lord has granted you the victory. You have been built and equipped for triumph. Take up your place on the battlefield and refuse to become a victim of the forces of darkness.

www.ingramcontent.com/pod-product-compliance
Lightning Source LLC
Chambersburg PA
CBHW030154100526

44592CB00009B/268